DAVID HARE

Amy's View

ff

faber and faber
LONDON · BOSTON

First published in 1997
by Faber and Faber Limited
3 Queen Square London WCIN 3AU

Typeset by Faber and Faber Ltd
Printed in England by Mackays of Chatham plc, Chatham, Kent

A CIP record for this book
is available from the British Library

ISBN 0-571-19179-7

David Hare was born in Sussex in 1947. His first play, *Slag*, was produced in 1970. A year later he first worked at the National Theatre, beginning one of the longest relationships of any playwright with a contemporary theatre. Since 1978, the National has produced eleven of his plays. Four of his best-known plays, *Plenty, The Secret Rapture, Racing Demon* and *Skylight*, have also been presented on Broadway. The first of his six feature films, *Wetherby*, which he also directed, won the Golden Bear at Berlin in 1985.

For Nicole,
pour toujours

Characters

Dominic Tyghe
Amy Thomas
Evelyn Thomas
Esme Allen
Frank Oddie
Toby Cole

Place
Near Pangbourne and in London.

Time
Between 1979 and 1995.

Amy's View was first performed at the Royal National Theatre's Lyttelton Theatre on 13 June 1997 with the following cast:

Dominic Tyghe Eoin McCarthy
Amy Thomas Samantha Bond
Evelyn Thomas Joyce Redmann
Esme Allen Judi Dench
Frank Oddie Ronald Pickup
Toby Cole Christopher Staines

Director Richard Eyre
Designer Bob Crowley
Lighting Mark Henderson
Music Richard Hartley

When shall we live, if not now?
Seneca

Act One

*The living room of a house in rural Berkshire, not far
from Pangbourne. The year is 1979. To one side there is a
large summerhouse-cum-veranda, full of plants. At the
back, a door leading to a hall and staircase. The room has
an air of exceptional taste, marked by the modern arts
movement of the 1920s and 30s. It is comfortable, with
sofas and chairs decked in attractively faded French fab-
rics. Nothing new has been bought for years. By the
biggest chair, discarded embroidery. This was once the
home of an artist, Bernard Thomas, and all round the
room is evidence of his work, which is rather Cezanne-like
and domestic in scale. There are small sculptures dotted
around. On one wall are some plates he designed. On
another, a box of objets trouvés. Yet the art is discreet,
part of the general surroundings, and plainly has been
there long enough to go unremarked.*

*It is past midnight, it is mid-summer, and it is pitch
dark outside. There are some warm orange standard
lamps on around the room and a lamp at a big table at
the back. In the centre of the room a striking-looking
young man, Dominic Tyghe, has turned a very old bicycle
upside down on some newspapers and is trying to mend
its front tyre. He has a big kitchen bowl of water to one
side. He is tall and thin, just twenty-two, with long black
hair, and is carelessly dressed like a student. Some way
apart, Amy Thomas, one year older, is sitting at the big
table. In front of her is a big pile of manuscripts which
she is assiduously working her way through, making tiny
notations. Dark-haired, in jeans and a T-shirt, she is also
thin, with an unmistakable air of quiet resolution.*

They are already talking as the play starts, caught in the middle of a chain of action.

Dominic I think it's this next.

Amy Do you want me to help you?

Dominic Can you remember?

Amy What do you do with the water? I do know you need it.

Dominic I know you need it. But I don't think I really know why.

Amy smiles across lovingly at his perplexed figure. Evelyn Thomas has come into the room. She is white-haired, in her late seventies, in good shape, but moving and talking in the self-contained rhythm of older people, on a course of her own. She is carrying in a pile of big books.

Evelyn I wanted to show him this album. Pictures of your mother when she was young.

Amy It is past midnight. Are you sure you shouldn't be going to bed?

Evelyn I wait every night.

Amy What time does she get here?

Dominic The talcum powder. The glue. The little rubber patch.

Evelyn It varies.

Dominic But in which order?

Amy The pub has already closed.

Evelyn has set the books down on the table, at the far end from Amy, and has started to look through them.

2

Evelyn Thank God your father never found this. Esme at RADA, some young man with his arm round her waist.

Amy Even if you manage to mend it, it's now too late for the beer.

Evelyn She comes in a taxi.

Amy What, from the station?

Evelyn Oh no. From London.

Amy My God!

Dominic It's no longer the beer. It's the challenge.

Evelyn is still turning the pages.

Evelyn Esme, with another young actress. Looking quite peaky.

Amy A taxi from London!

Dominic It's the sense of achievement I want.

Evelyn looks up a moment.

Evelyn You did tell her you were coming?

Amy I left a message. Some woman at the theatre. She sounded sort of ginny. Three packs a day.

Evelyn Yes. That's her dresser. Tweed skirts. A voice like Alvar Lidell.

Amy That was her.

Evelyn Did you mention your friend?

Amy Not by name. But I did say I was two.

Evelyn She'll be pleased to see you. She never sees anyone. Of course, she pretends that she does. I suppose she does see the neighbours. But I wouldn't count them.

Amy Nor would I.

Evelyn Horses and hip operations, otherwise you're wasting your time. (*She turns another page.*) Here she is again, looking sluttish.

Amy has gone over to see how Dominic's getting on.

Amy This little rubber sticker, it goes there . . . no, first it goes in the liquid.

Dominic Do you think it's just been in the garage too long?

Evelyn That's Bernard's bicycle.

Amy We thought it must be.

Evelyn For a start, he's been dead fifteen years. And he didn't cycle for another fifteen before that.

Dominic Oh then, I must say, no wonder.

Evelyn Overall, you may be looking back to the war.

Dominic laughs at the hopelessness of it.

Dominic Yes, well, whoever, they lost the instructions.

Evelyn Are you sure you have the right one? I could never tell the difference between the John Bull bicycle repair kit and that little printing set they do as well.

Amy Oh yes, of course . . .

Dominic holds up the metal tin.

Dominic There's a man in a Union Jack waistcoat . . .

Amy . . . the printing set!

Evelyn That's not conclusive.

Amy The time I spent getting my fingers bright blue . . . with those little rubber ants . . .

4

Evelyn Ah yes. Your paper.

Amy, going back to the table, raises her voice for the older woman.

Amy You remember? I did it for years. You can't have forgotten. How could you? Surely. It was called *Amy's View*.

Evelyn So it was.

Amy You see. Infant journalist. Crosswords. Cartoons. Interviews. Mostly with my mother, I'm afraid. I used to hawk it round the widows of Pangbourne. I made a small fortune.

Dominic And what have you done with the money?

Amy Oh, sure. Spent. All spent.

Dominic Well, we could do with it now.

Evelyn has gone back to the album.

Evelyn Esme, smiling at the seaside. Wearing an unfortunate jumper.

Dominic (*sniffing*) Do you think people used these things to get high? (*He goes to glue the rubber strip at the table.*)

Amy Dominic was spared all the pleasures of family. He was brought up by nuns.

Dominic Well, not exactly.

Evelyn What's she saying?

Dominic (*raising his voice*) I'm an orphan.

Evelyn I'm sorry.

Dominic There's really no need.

Evelyn speaks as if Dominic were not present.

Evelyn Does he know who his parents are?

Amy No.

Dominic I always thought they'd turn out to be frightful. And not to be interested in the same things as me. I'm not sure we'd know what to say to one another.

Evelyn Wouldn't you?

Dominic Apart from 'Oh, so it's you'. (*He seems unperturbed.*) I don't think it's really such a big issue. They're strangers. I don't think they marked me for life.

Evelyn Don't you?

Dominic No. No, I don't think so. I just am who I am. (*He frowns a moment at the table.*) I do know they're poor. I believe they weren't married. I think someone once told me my mother had died. I mean, died having me. But how would I know without asking?

Evelyn What a strange thing for your young man to say.

Amy is unsettled by Evelyn's reaction.

Amy Is it? I understand.

Evelyn Do you?

Amy Of course. His family didn't want him. That's what they were saying by letting him go. They were saying, we're sorry, but we actually want to get rid of you . . .

Evelyn More likely they weren't able to cope.

Amy Yes, that as well. Of course, that's part of it. At least I would guess it was. And of course, it's not for us to judge why they did what they did. But. It seems clear to me Dominic also has rights. And if he decides he'd rather not know anything . . . (*She suddenly stops, embarrassed.*) Well, *you* say, Dominic. No, really. It's your life, not mine.

6

Dominic Obviously, I can only guess at their reasons. But it's always seemed to me like they made a choice.

Amy Well, that's right.

Dominic I have to allow them that choice. Why should I get back in touch with them if it means I may risk getting hurt?

Evelyn looks at him quite sharply.

Evelyn What a depressing philosophy. Are you sure you're with the right man?

Amy Quite sure.

Dominic I don't think she's worried.

Evelyn Of course not. At her age, that's par for the course.

Dominic has gone back to the bike, not taking this mischief-making seriously.

Amy Grandma, we don't need your views on the subject . . .

Evelyn I'm saying nothing. I'm reading this book.

Amy Good. So I should hope.

Dominic is kneeling, putting on the blue strip.

Amy All right, Dominic?

Dominic Why, sure. Everything's fine. (*He spins the wheel, the job done.*)

Amy Dominic's editing a film magazine. That's his main interest. He writes about films.

Evelyn In my day we just used to watch them.

Dominic Ah yes, but things have moved on.

Amy Evelyn taught art . . .

Evelyn I did.

Amy In a school . . .

Evelyn In the same school. Quite near here. For over forty years. I always told the children: just do it. What is there to say?

Amy Ah well, Dominic doesn't feel that at all.

Evelyn No.

Dominic I think it's worth while to discuss the whole concept of cinema. To work out what cinema is. It is so extraordinary. I can't get past this extraordinary idea. That actually it's nothing. Finally it's nothing. It's just beams of light. And yet. (*He stands a moment, thinking it through.*) All that complexity, that feeling. And it's all in the air.

Amy You should read what he's written. He has these extraordinary theories . . .

Dominic (*modestly*) Well . . .

Amy To do with psychology. The relation of cinema to dream. He's worked out a system of what he calls dominant symbols . . .

Dominic Signifiers, some people say . . .

Amy And he relates them to how we experience fictive narratives while sleeping. I know it sounds heavy, but when you read it, it makes perfect sense.

Evelyn is neutral, giving nothing away.

Evelyn What's it called, this magazine?

Dominic *Noir et Blanc.*

Amy It's in English. It's just the title that's French.

Evelyn Well, good.

Amy Dominic started it himself. I go round in the evening . . .

Dominic There's only two of us.

Amy I go round selling in cafés, in cinemas . . .

Evelyn I thought you'd got a job of your own.

Amy Yes. But this is the evenings. I go out and sell *Noir et Blanc*. (*She stops, as if brought up short.*) It's odd. It hadn't occurred to me. It's like *Amy's View*.

Evelyn Yes.

Amy Except this time the view is Dominic's. (*Before she has time to be embarrassed she hears an approaching taxi.*) Is that the sound of a car?

Evelyn Did you say she's coming?

Amy Dominic, I think it's my mother.

Evelyn I'll put her food in the oven. The pub sends something round.

Dominic I'll move the bike.

Evelyn It's usually disgusting.

Amy My goodness, she gets her food from the pub?

Evelyn has gone. Seeing Dominic about to move the bike, Amy stops him.

There's no need. You mustn't be embarrassed. She's terribly easy, I promise you that.

Dominic It's all right. It's not me that's embarrassed.

Amy No.

Dominic kisses her lightly. They wait a moment, their backs to us, like children. Then we see Amy take his hand.

Esme (*off*) Hello. Is there anyone there?

Amy (*raising her voice*) Yes. Yes. We're in here.

Esme Allen comes in. She is forty-nine, in a simple dress and carrying a big bag. She is surprisingly small, her manner both sensitive and intense. Something in her vulnerability makes people instantly protective of her.

Esme Amy, how are you? How good to see you. Are you all right? You don't look very well.

Amy No, I'm fine.

Esme kisses and hugs her daughter warmly.

Mother, I promised I'd introduce you. This is my friend with a bike.

Esme We've never met.

Dominic No.

They shake hands. There is a slight hiatus.

Dominic.

Esme How are you?

Dominic Thank you. I'm very well.

They both smile at their own awkwardness. Evelyn comes in and starts laying a place.

Esme I got your message. I'm thrilled at this privilege.

Dominic Just let me move this.

Esme Don't move it, please, on my account. I quite like it there. What've you been doing? Rallying?

Amy No, Mother, he's just been mending the tyre.

Dominic has turned the tyre upright and is leaning it against the wall.

Esme I see. Is he freelance? Does he do fuses and plugs? The tank in the attic's in a terrible state. Why did he start with the bike?

Amy Very funny . . .

Esme I don't need to bother with supper, Evelyn.

Amy He fancied the pub for a beer.

But Evelyn is already on her way out.

Esme Tell me, how long are you down for?

Amy Oh, well that's up to Dominic. I got a couple of days from my publishing house.

Esme Did you get some dinner? I'm afraid there's never anything here. Evelyn's gone macrobiotic or something. She eats pulses. She believes they're prolonging her life. As if it hadn't gone on long enough.

Dominic There we are.

Esme I get in steak and kidney if I'm not to starve.

Amy smiles in recognition of Evelyn.

Amy Yes, Evelyn's already cast an eye over Dominic. Found fault with him.

Esme No! She's insane.

Amy That's what I think.

Esme In Pangbourne, for God's sake. A man under fifty

who can actually handle a spanner! Leave him outside the door and he'd be snapped up in a trice.

Dominic seems happy with the flattery.

So. What do you do? Amy says you're a journalist . . .

Dominic Oh, well yes, of a kind.

Esme What kind?

Dominic I've started a magazine. Also I write bits for a diary. For a national paper. Just to make money.

Amy It's only what he's doing for now.

Dominic That's right.

Esme What sort of diary?

Dominic The usual sort. We ring people up and we're terribly nice to them. Then we write something horrid which appears the next day. At least that's the general procedure.

Esme Ah. And you don't ever get the two bits confused? Find yourself being horrid in person? Then accidentally writing something nice the next day . . .

Dominic Oh no, that would be gross professional misconduct. You'd be hounded out of Fleet Street for that.

They share the joke, but it worries Amy.

I mean, no, in fact . . .

Amy No, really . . .

Esme I'm joking.

Dominic Me too. I'm being facetious. The diary's a way of just getting by. At least until I can do what I want.

Esme Which is?

Dominic It sounds silly even to say. But I suppose eventually I want to make films.

There is a moment's silence.

Esme Ah, right then. Why is that silly?

Dominic Isn't it what everyone wants?

Esme If you want it enough, I've no doubt you'll do it.

Dominic Yes. That's what Amy says.

Esme watches, realizing how serious it is between them.

Actually, the diary's been terribly interesting.

Esme Really?

Dominic Yes, I've been quite impressed.

Esme walks across the room to sit in a big armchair. Dominic is more confident.

At first I was scared. I was talking to such famous people. Especially film people. We'd talk on the phone, I'd write down what they say. Blah blah blah. But then I noticed, if I write something praiseful, they feel sort of grateful.

Esme Why, surely.

Dominic Yes, but I think I've been quite surprised.

Esme Why?

Dominic Well, just . . . these are well-known people. You think perhaps by now they'd be more secure. But not at all. No, you write as if you like them and suddenly they're really responsive.

Esme Of course.

Dominic Yes, but it almost shocks me how much.

Esme is looking at him a little harder.

Esme So what are you saying?

Dominic I don't know. I suppose in my little way . . . just on this stupid diary, I mean . . . I suppose I've realized that writing is power.

Esme Uh-huh. Which you can use consciously?

Dominic Sort of.

Esme So you can start to advance your career?

She has not said it unkindly but it prompts a rush of denial from them both.

Dominic Well . . .

Amy Dominic doesn't mean that.

Dominic No. Not at all.

Amy Dominic'd never do that.

Dominic No. Not blatantly. But on the other hand, if you take what they say – which is often not interesting – and you make it witty, next day you give it some oomph, then I've noticed they call you. It's a hideous phrase, but you begin to make contacts.

Amy And that's something which Dominic realizes he may have to do.

Esme Make contacts?

Dominic Yes.

Esme Goodness.

Dominic I can't avoid it. If I'm to make films. And why not?

Amy Yes. You're just getting access.

Dominic That's it. (*There is a slight silence.*) The mistake, of course, would be to take the stuff I write seriously. But what does it matter? As we say on the diary, it's gone in a day.

Esme Mmm.

Esme has grown thoughtful. Amy wants to dispel the atmosphere.

Amy I hadn't realized the play was still running.

Esme No, well it was going to close. Then someone re-opened it. In a smaller theatre.

Amy I see. And you're still in it?

Esme Oh yes. At least for a while.

Amy joins in the familiar complaint.

Esme and Amy There are no parts for women.

Esme I have a good death scene at least. The writer's not terribly present. Nor the director. They only stay for the opening.

Amy They wind you up and you go.

Esme Yes.

Esme tucks her legs up under her and looks absently at Evelyn who has returned.

What on earth are you doing with that album?

Evelyn I got it out to show it to Amy's young friend. But he showed no interest.

Esme No, well he's right. There's nothing to see.

Amy looks anxiously to Dominic.

Amy Dominic, you've never seen my mother acting.

15

Dominic No. It must seem ridiculous. I do know how famous you are. But my generation . . . by and large, we don't go to the theatre. To us it doesn't seem relevant.

Esme Now why should it? I quite understand.

Evelyn goes out again, saying nothing.

Esme People say, 'Oh, everyone should go to the theatre.' Why should they? We don't want an audience being brought in by force. And for us, there's nothing more disheartening than playing to people who are there because they've been told it's doing them good.

Dominic Quite.

Esme Let's play to people who actually like it. And if there aren't very many, so be it. But don't come because you've been told to. No, that won't do at all.

She is thoughtful, so again Amy prompts her to cheer her up.

Amy Mummy is brilliant at playing comedy.

Esme I'm usually best at playing genteel. With something interesting happening underneath. Layers. I play lots of layers.

Amy She plays them wonderfully.

Esme Thank you. My Shakespearean heroines were not a success. I suffered with a gay Orlando. Amy remembers. Everything was fine when I was dressed as a boy.

Amy But then there's this bit . . . *As You Like It*, do you know? She has to reveal she's a woman . . .

Esme He was right. I don't blame him. I was sexier the other way.

Amy Nonsense!

16

Esme But, oh dear! The look on his face . . . (*She lights a cigarette.*)

Amy It was funny.

Dominic Did it show?

Esme Theatre's a young person's game. Eventually it becomes undignified. Dressing up, pretending to be someone else. Then saying things which someone else tells you to. After a while you start to think, where am I? Where do I fit in all of this?

Amy consciously keeps things going.

Amy How are the rest of them? How is that actor? The one who plays the old man.

Esme Oh, they've changed him. Now Perry Potter is playing that part. You know Perry. He wears a scarf. And a sort of *pain bagnat* to cover his baldness.

Amy A *pain bagnat*?

Esme You know those things. Like this. (*She swirls her hand round her head.*)

Amy What on earth are you talking about? A *pain bagnat* is a kind of a sandwich.

Esme Why . . .

Amy With olives and tuna. Mother, it comes in a bun.

Esme Of course, I know that. I know that!

Amy She has such extraordinary gaps in her knowledge. She thinks a *pain bagnat* is a hat!

Esme Oh, very satirical. You're all so superior. With your new universities. I don't have book learning, not the hyper-accurate type. But I have a different kind of intelligence . . .

Amy Oh yes, we all know that kind of intelligence. The kind that's kind of like just being thick.

Evelyn returns with salt and pepper and a half-drunk bottle of wine.

Esme I had irregular schooling. Ask Evelyn. Schools didn't teach in those days. It was considered vulgar.

Amy They taught. But you chose not to hear.

Dominic is politely interested.

Dominic Do you do television also?

Esme Oh, television, really!

Amy She hates it.

Esme I do.

Amy She doesn't even watch.

Esme Working your guts out while people do something else. There you are, working. What are they doing? Eating. Or talking. Just great! Being taken no notice of in ten million homes.

They all smile. Esme seems more comfortable now.

Dominic Do you always come back in the evening?

Esme When Amy was young, I just hated to leave her. She was such a sweet girl. She always filled this house with her friends.

Amy My girlfriends used to sleep over.

Esme And then I suppose I got used to it. I still don't like sleeping in London.

Amy She doesn't like staying there after a show.

Esme That's right. It's the nature of my job. It's all opinion.

People flitting round telling you 'I like it, I don't. I thought this, I didn't think that.' There's nothing to get hold of. But at least if I come home in the evening . . . well, I just like the feeling. I look at this house and something is real.

She looks round a moment. Evelyn is still pottering.

I don't want to eat, Evelyn.

Amy Grandma, you should be going to bed.

Evelyn Why? I'll sleep when I'm dead.

Esme Television? No I don't want to do it. For as long as London has its fabled West End . . .

She stubs out her cigarette. Evelyn goes out again.

And you?

Amy Oh, I'm fine. Really. We just fancied a visit. And of course for you to meet Dominic too.

Dominic responds tactfully.

Dominic Here. Let me take this bike to the garage.

Amy Well, thank you.

Dominic I'll be back in a mo.

He goes out. The two women are alone.

Esme You'd better say. I'm not such a bad mother.

Amy What?

Esme Not such a bad mother that I can't tell. Please, I don't think I can stand an engagement. Do people still do that?

Amy No. I promise that's not what this is.

Esme Well?

Amy It's not serious. I promise you, it's nothing serious at all. I'm wanting to borrow some money.

Esme Ah, thank goodness. Money, that's all. (*She seems genuinely relieved.*) Of course. How much do you need?

Amy I'd like five thousand.

Esme I'm sorry?

Amy That would be perfect.

Esme Say that again. (*She suddenly looks at Amy directly.*) Why on earth do you want five thousand? There's nothing in the world which costs five thousand pounds.

Amy If you don't mind, I don't want to say.

Esme I'm glad, in that case, it's not serious. What would have been serious? Ten?

Amy I will tell you. I promise I will tell you one day. But you've always said: if I needed anything I was to come to you.

Esme Why, surely.

Amy No strings attached. Well, Mother, I'm here.

Esme recognizes a note of challenge and rises to it.

Esme That's fine. That's no problem. Now? How do you want it? Do you want a cheque?

Amy If you could.

Esme Sure. Yes, of course. Let me do it. Now where exactly did I put my things?

Amy There. Behind you.

Esme Of course. (*She takes her bag across to the table.*) How much?

Amy Five thousand.

Esme You mean five thousand pounds? Do you mean all in one go? Not in instalments? One day you will give it back?

Amy smiles politely at these jokes. Esme has opened her cheque book.

Amy You always said, if ever . . . if ever something came up, you wouldn't ask anything, you'd simply give me whatever I asked.

Esme Oh yes. (*She pauses a second.*) But first just tell me what this something is.

Amy Mum . . .

Esme No, really, I'm joking. I trust you. You know I do. I'm not asking anything. Not a thing. I know if I asked you would tell me, but I'm not going to ask. (*She starts writing. Amy just watches.*) Which account is it? I have no idea. There's money from Bernard's estate. Well, something. The ludicrous thing is, I don't make anything at all from the play. I'm losing. By the time I've got a taxi from London, I don't have anything left. (*She looks up at Amy.*) Now what is the date?

Amy June 25th. It's 1979.

Esme Well, I know that. Please, do you think I live in a dream? (*She hands Amy the cheque.*)

Amy Thank you.

Esme How did I do?

Amy Brilliantly.

Esme Aren't you proud of your Mum? Cash it quickly before it can bounce. No, really. You're fine. It'll pay. (*She kisses Amy.*) The Trappist. I shan't say any more. (*She* *starts opening doors and calling out.*) Now, Dominic, are you all right? Are you lost in the garage? Evelyn, what's happened? What's going on? Perhaps I will have the cottage pie after all. I'm emotionally exhausted. Two minutes alone with my daughter and I've lost a whole lot of calories.

Both Dominic and Evelyn have reappeared, Evelyn with shrivelled pub dinner.

Ah, Dominic, right, there you are.

Dominic I am.

Esme Are you going to bed, the two of you?

Dominic Soon.

Amy slips the cheque among her things and looks to see what Dominic is doing.

I have to write something first.

Evelyn (*putting down the plate*) Here it is.

Esme My God, what have you done to it? Vegetarian's revenge. The way she heats it! Every day less attractive, until I give in.

Evelyn It's pure crap.

Esme I know. I love it. Do we have any HP?

Amy has been looking to contact Dominic.

Amy Are you going up?

Dominic I'll just work a little.

Amy Shall I come with you?

Dominic Do you mind? Just give me ten minutes. For God's sake, I just need ten minutes, all right? Is that so unreasonable?

He has snapped at her. Suddenly the atmosphere is tense.

Amy No, of course not. No problem.

Dominic stops, trying to take the heat out of the moment.

Dominic I'll see you later. Goodnight, Esme.

Esme Goodnight.

Dominic goes out. Esme has her meal in front of her, but makes no effort to start.

Well, there it is. It's extraordinary. You've found yourself such a handsome young man.

Amy Why? Does that surprise you?

Esme Not in the slightest. Any man's lucky to end up with you.

The tone of this is light and friendly but Amy is ill at ease.

The theatre, of course, is full of these people. Good-looking young men who have yet to find out who they are. I see them all the time.

Amy Is that meant to be Dominic?

Esme Well, you know him better than me.

Esme waits but Amy says nothing.

But, on the other hand, you have come to ask my opinion . . .

Amy Have I?

Esme I think so.

Amy I'd say on the contrary. Didn't I ask you not to say a word?

Esme Amy, please, I wasn't born yesterday. When a daughter comes to her mother and says, 'Don't ask anything, I beg you, ask nothing at all . . .', isn't it just a way of saying, 'Quick, Mother, help! I'm desperate to talk'?

Amy can't resist smiling at this.

Amy Are you saying I did that unconsciously?

Esme Unconsciously? Hardly. 'Give me five thousand pounds.' As a way of getting my attention, it would take some beating. Well, wouldn't it?

Amy Yes. I don't know. Oh perhaps. I'm confused. (*She smiles, relaxing, giving in.*)

Esme After all that is the basic skill. That *is* my profession. You have to get that right or you might as well give up. You say one thing but you're thinking another. If you can't do that, then truly you shouldn't be doing the job.

A look of mischief comes onto Amy's face.

Amy That reminds me, I did see that thing with Deirdre . . .

Esme Oh, Deirdre!

Amy I saw that new play which stars Deirdre Keane.

Esme Well, Deirdre can't even manage the line in the first place, let alone the bit where you think something else.

Amy She wasn't very good.

Esme They tell me she's laughable. Apparently she comes on, dressed like a lampshade, a great smear of lipstick right across her face . . .

Amy They're right . . .

Esme They say, rolling her eyes like a demented puppy-

24

dog and facing out front all the time. (*She is shaking her head as if outraged.*)

Amy She got very good reviews.

Esme Deirdre? She practically goes down on the critics. You've seen her. She's craven. She's always trying to please.

Amy Is that such a bad thing?

Esme Of course not. But nobody's explained to her the basis of the whole project.

Amy Which is?

Esme Why, to please without seeming to try.

Amy Oh, I see.

Esme That's what one's attempting. Of course, we all know it can't be achieved. But that's the ideal. To make it look effortless. (*Esme looks at Amy a moment.*) Perhaps it applies just as much in our lives.

Amy looks, knowing she cannot avoid things any longer.

Amy Look, Mum, I do know you're desperate to talk to me . . .

Esme Me?

Amy There's a thousand questions you're longing to ask . . .

Esme I can see you're in trouble. In a moment I'm hoping you're going to say why.

Amy It's not trouble. I wouldn't say trouble exactly . . .

Esme How's life in your publishing firm?

Amy Great. They're trying to promote me.

Esme I'm pleased.

Amy But one thing's bound up in another.

25

Amy stops dead. Esme speaks quietly.

Esme You're expecting a child?

Amy How did you know? Is it really that obvious?

Esme It isn't not obvious.

Amy When did you know?

Esme The moment I saw you, of course.

Esme pushes her uneaten meal aside. She gets up and takes Amy in her arms. Amy can barely speak through her tears.

Amy Oh God, I'm going to cry . . .

Esme Well, cry. (*She begins to sob with Amy.*) Please cry, cry all you want to . . .

Amy No, no, I mustn't . . .

Esme Oh, Amy . . .

Amy I mustn't . . . (*She tears herself decisively away.*)

Esme Why not? It's wonderful . . .

Amy I mustn't!

Esme Amy, this is wonderful news.

Amy Because . . . oh shit, I don't know how to say this. You're going to think I'm insane. (*She is wild, raising her voice.*) I haven't told Dominic. I know this sounds crazy but I don't think I shall.

Before Esme can react, Evelyn appears again, beating her usual path.

Evelyn You haven't eaten your supper.

Esme No. Why don't you go to your bed?

Evelyn What's wrong with her? Why is she crying?

Esme Hay fever.

Evelyn Do you want me to re-heat it?

Esme No thank you.

Evelyn has gone over to collect the plate. Esme raises her voice to Evelyn.

Esme I don't think it can take any more.

Evelyn (*to Amy*) You know she doesn't eat **anything**.

Amy Oh really?

Evelyn She comes in here, looks at it, then pushes the plate to one side.

Esme has moved across to usher her out.

Esme Evelyn, you must go, you must go to **your** bed now.

Evelyn I'm not going to sleep.

Esme Very well then. Just lie. Just lie there. Think about family. Here we are. Under one roof. The whole of our family. At least such as it is. Think about that and be grateful. (*She kisses Evelyn.*)

Evelyn Just promise me she's not going to marry the critic.

Amy I promise you, Grandma.

Evelyn If she's not going to marry the critic, then I think I can sleep.

Evelyn goes out, pleased with having said it. Esme and Amy are both amused at the absurdity.

Esme Oh, Amy . . .

Amy Well, really! She never changes.

Esme No.

Amy She seems really well.

Esme Oh, sure. She's going to outlive me. It doesn't bother me. I've known that for years. (*She goes and gets her cigarettes.*) It's become a marriage, like any other. If, when I'd met Bernard, they'd said to me, you'll live ten years longer with Bernard's mother than you will with Bernard himself . . . I'm not sure I'd have jumped in so eagerly. (*She lights her cigarette.*) But you never know how things are going to turn out.

Amy No.

Esme looks at her a moment.

Esme So what is the problem? Dominic's the father?

Amy Oh yes. We can say that for sure.

Esme But you feel – what? – for some reason that now's not the moment for Dominic to know?

Amy Exactly.

Esme I see. Well, it's interesting. It makes for an original decision. But I can't help feeling there's some sort of flaw in the reasoning perhaps. You're hoping he's not going to notice?

Amy No. No, of course not . . .

Esme You don't feel it's possible he's going to find out?

Amy is amused, but Esme goes on.

I mean, I do see the man is an egghead. But even so you'd have to be pretty unworldly!

Amy You know very well that's not what I mean.

Esme Do I?

Amy now sees a way to explain.

Amy It's true. He *is* an intellectual. But in some ways he's younger than me. In a sense, he's a bit like a child. In a good way. He's childlike, is that the word?

Esme Childlike is good. Childish is less good.

Amy Yes. In that case, the first.

Esme is just watching, not commenting.

But also the thing is . . . he's extremely attractive.

Esme Ah.

Amy It's something . . . well, it makes things different, I find.

Esme Yes, I can see. The little-boy manner . . .

Amy For instance, we met at a publishing party. Dominic arrived with this girl. She was only eighteen. And she'd published a novel. I have to say, not a bad novel . . .

Esme Oh, novels!

Amy And what's more she had these incredible legs . . .

Esme Ah, well then . . .

Amy Jet-black hair. This wonderful bosom. I saw them as soon as they walked in the room. All the time they were laughing together, her arm around him, like she didn't have a care in the world. (*She stops a moment.*) So yes, I admit, it slightly surprised me when he came over. When he started talking to me.

Esme And how did she take it?

Amy The teenage novelist? Well, I think she felt pretty miffed. I think they all are. The tall one. The blonde one from Cambridge. Another one who sang in a band . . .

Esme And it's the thought of these ex-s which is unsettling you . . .

Amy No, not exactly. Oh God, I'm explaining this badly . . .

Esme Don't tell me you think you can't compete.

Amy Not at all. No. I do know what I'm giving him. I'm giving something none of the others could give.

Esme What's that?

Amy Self-confidence. I give him some faith in himself. I build him up.

Esme Yes, I'm sure. And what exactly is he giving you?

Amy begins to sound defensive.

Amy Look . . .

Esme No, I mean it . . .

Amy Now, Mother . . .

Esme You're telling me you're flattered. As you describe him, he has women around him like flies. And you're thinking, 'And he's chosen me! Golly Moses! I'm going to do anything to hold on to this . . .'

Amy Mother, that isn't fair.

Esme To a point where you're frightened to tell him you're pregnant! Is that it? You're frightened you'll lose him. Is that how things are? (*She turns away, deeply disturbed.*) Oh, Amy, I can't believe it. I'm shocked. This is terrible . . .

Amy Really, I promise you, that's not it at all.

Esme Isn't it? You've given me a list of his conquests.

What am I meant to say? Me, I don't care who he's slept with. He's buggered the Dagenham Girl Pipers. So? All I care is what happens to you.

Amy Of course.

Esme If he loves you.

Amy Of course.

Esme Does he say it?

Amy Oh really!

Esme I mean it. In those exact words?

Amy Yes. Yes, he has said it.

Esme Good. I know it's meant to be just the first step. You expect to go on from there. But the fact is, in my experience, it's quite alarming how few of them can even do that.

Now it is Amy's turn to be angry.

Amy All right, for God's sake, he says it! He says it. Why are you so worried?

Esme Why am I worried? Why on earth do you think?

Amy (*conceding*) All right . . .

Esme What a question!

Amy All right!

Esme You seem to think just because this man is attractive it somehow absolves him from doing what any normal, decent person should do.

Amy tries to give her a real explanation.

Amy No, that's not it. I have to explain to you. There are things . . . there's a background you don't yet understand.

31

But the point is, Mother, you do have to listen . . .

Esme I'm listening . . .

Amy You have to sit down and promise to give me a chance.

Esme Well of course.

Amy I've lived through this nightmare. Now I'm beginning to see a way through. But you must give me a hearing.

Esme Why, surely.

Amy Without interruption.

Esme Amy, I hope I've always done that. (*She looks reproachful.*)

Amy The truth is . . . my relationship with Dominic has been pretty fragile. It's volatile, is that the word? He can be bad-tempered. He suffers from depression quite badly. At times he . . . well, he's like . . . he's a victim of moods.

Esme is silent, her disapproval clear.

So, the point is, I thought, this is really tricky. Do I just go to him and tell him outright? No, that's going to shock him. And also . . . I know for a fact he will say to me, look, will I get rid of it?

Esme Amy . . .

Amy And, for me, there's no question of that. So, all right. It's like solving a puzzle. I want to keep the baby and I want to keep Dominic as well. So I must work out a way of telling him so he doesn't feel pressured, so he doesn't feel, 'Oh God, this is just what I feared . . .'

Esme is becoming restless.

He said . . . he has said from the start he wasn't ready for children . . .

Esme Oh really!

Amy Mother!

Esme All right . . .

Amy He said this. From the very first day. The point is, I made him a promise. No children. He said: 'Whatever else, I can't face starting a family . . .' (*She stops a moment.*) So you must see that does make things difficult now.

But Esme cannot stay quiet.

Esme What was this? Some sort of contract?

Amy Mum . . .

Esme Some sort of written agreement which he had you sign?

Amy No.

Esme Without any allowance for what might actually happen?

Amy Mother, you promised!

Esme Yes. I promised to give you a hearing. Not to let you throw away your whole life! (*She stubs out her cigarette and gets up.*) This stuff: no children! It's abstract! It's all in the abstract!

Amy I know.

Esme But something has happened. It's actually happened. An event which changes all that. You are actually having the baby. Whether he likes it or not, the baby exists.

Amy Yes, of course. So?

Esme *So*, I'd have thought it was obvious, the sooner you face him, the sooner you tell him . . .

Amy No. That's where you're wrong. Because I just know – I can feel in my stomach – it's going to seem like it's blackmail.

Esme Oh, come now!

Amy For him it'll be like I'm springing a trap. (*She suddenly raises her voice.*) It's everything he's feared! I know him. You don't. I tell him now and at once he's going to feel cornered . . .

Esme That is ridiculous! What kind of man is this?

Amy And when Dominic feels cornered, I tell you, I've seen him, he turns just incredibly stubborn and ugly . . .

Esme Well then, you've answered my question.

Amy Mother, I'm sorry, but I'm very clear about this. (*She is reluctant, not wanting to go on.*) The fact is . . . you know . . . I'd not wanted to tell you . . . the girl from Cambridge . . . the one who was with him before . . . the point is she also . . . she also got pregnant.

Esme Ah. Now I see what you're telling me. (*She has stopped as if at last seeing to the heart of Amy's problems.*) And I suppose we can guess what happened to her.

Amy shifts uncomfortably.

Amy Oh, look, I mean it's not . . . it wasn't immediate. It wasn't like, 'She's pregnant, I'm off . . .'

Esme No?

Amy But it's true. He stopped her having the baby. Then

34

he told me things did start to sour between them. And, pretty soon after, he felt that he'd had enough.

Esme looks hard at Amy.

Esme But, Amy . . .

Amy I know . . .

Esme You do have to ask yourself . . .

Amy I know, Mother. I know what you're going to say. But the answer is: yes. He is the right man for me. I know this. I know it profoundly. In a way which is way beyond anything.

Esme is silenced by Amy's conviction.

So it's just a question of what I do now.

Esme sits down quietly at the table.

Amy That's why I came to you and asked for the money. The money will mean I can be by myself. That means . . . well, if I have to, I can bring up the baby alone. Of course I will tell him. I'll tell him eventually. After some months. But what I will not do is bully him into some sort of disastrous alliance – out of sheer circumstance – when the point is, it's not what he wants.

Esme And what you want, does that count for nothing?

Amy Yes, of course it's important. I promise you, I've thought this thing through. I charge in, I frighten him. Where does that get me? All that happens is I destroy the whole thing. (*She reaches across and takes Esme's hand.*) You always said I was the rational one in the family. I was blessed with certainty, that's what you said.

Esme Yes I did.

Amy So please, you must trust me. It's a matter of timing.

35

And the timing is something which I must decide.

Dominic appears at the door. He has a pad of paper on which he has been writing.

Dominic Oh, I see. Lord, you're still talking . . .

Amy Dominic, my goodness . . .

Dominic Have I butted in?

Amy No. Not at all. Not in the slightest.

Amy looks nervously to Esme. Dominic is aware of the atmosphere.

We were just chatting. Discussing old times.

Dominic I realized I can't find the books that I needed. Do you know if they're in your case?

Amy Oh, sure. Let me get them.

Dominic No, don't be silly.

Amy No really, I know where they are.

Dominic If you're sure.

Amy It won't take two seconds. All right, then, Mother? I'll be back in a sec.

Amy squeezes her hand, then goes out. Esme doesn't move. The wine is unopened in front of her. Dominic starts to look round the room.

Dominic It's nice here.

Esme I'm sorry?

Dominic The house.

Esme Oh.

Dominic It's beautiful. The pictures. Your husband did

these? What is it, this one? Oil on canvas? (*He is looking closely at one of the oils.*) The cross-hatch technique. Is that what it's called? Eggshell. Amy told me he was an artist. I like the style very much. What is it called?

Esme Called?

Dominic What school was he part of?

Esme What school?

Dominic What movement?

Esme I suppose he gets lumped as an English impressionist. At least, when they auction him, that's what he's called. But Bernard didn't call himself anything.

Dominic Oh really?

Esme No. I don't know how to explain this, but it's simply not how he thought.

Amy appears, with a couple of film reference books under her arm. She looks to see nothing untoward has occurred.

Amy Here we are.

Dominic Oh, thanks.

Amy I'll come up with you. You don't mind if I read?

Dominic No.

Amy I'll say goodnight then. (*She leans down to Esme and kisses her.*) Mother, goodnight.

Esme gets up and moves towards the door.

Esme Dominic, my daughter has something to tell you. In my view, it's essential she speaks to you tonight. So I'm leaving you here and I'm going to bed. (*She stops for a split second at the door.*) She's pregnant.

Esme goes out. It has all happened so quickly that Amy is lost for a response. Then she runs out into the corridor where we can see her calling upstairs.

Amy Why did you tell him? Mum, what the hell's going on?

Act Two

The same. Six years later. It is a Saturday afternoon in late July. The year is 1985. It is towards the end of a perfect summer day. Benign sunshine is flooding into the room from the windows and from the greenhouse and veranda at the back. Although so much time has gone by, the room appears identical.

Esme comes through the door, wearing a slightly ostentatious satin outfit with a floral motif, and a rather extravagant hat. She is carrying gloves, a bag and a huge bundle of flowers. Although now fifty-five, she is also little changed. Amy is immediately behind her, once more in jeans and a simple shirt. She is only twenty-nine, but motherhood and the passage of her twenties has made a mark on her. She is more confident but her hair is tied more austerely, and there is a wariness, a sense of strain.

Both of the women are in exceptionally high spirits, an ordeal behind them. As at the beginning of Act One, the action is already in train as the lights come up.

Esme Let me take off this hat.

Amy Oh, the hat was just crazy.

Esme Oh, flowers! What flowers!

Esme puts the flowers down on the table to take off her hat. The room is muggy with the day's heat, so Amy goes to open the greenhouse doors.

I knew from the start the hat was *de trop*.

Amy Well, it was. People could hardly see past it. All they could see was this enormous saucer on top of your head.

Bright green. Even your face looked iridescent.

Esme Well, thank you.

Amy kisses Esme.

Amy Nobody can say you don't give it a go.

Esme But I carried the gloves, did you notice? I never put them on. That was the clever touch.

Amy I should hope not. Who are you? The bloody Queen Mother?

Esme No. Just auditioning.

They both smile at the truth of this.

Did you see Evelyn?

Amy It's all right. She's sleeping.

Esme Well, come on then, Frank, are you going to come in?

Frank Oh, thank you.

Frank Oddie is hanging around the doorway, but now comes in. In his early fifties, he looks easy-going and amiable in his shirtsleeves, tie and flannels. He carries his jacket. His manner is a touch apologetic, as if out of his natural habitat. Esme passes him as she goes out to hang up her hat and kick off her shoes.

Esme (*from the hall*) Did we lose Dominic?

Amy He's taking care of the children.

Esme For once.

Frank, in the middle of the room, loudly addresses no one in particular.

Frank Oh, God, all that lemonade!

40

Amy I told him he had to. For once he's bloody well got to.

Esme I just hope he wasn't too bored. (*She has come back barefoot and is unwrapping the flowers on the table.*) I couldn't tell behind those dark glasses.

Frank Now can we drink something serious?

Esme He has wonderful dark glasses.

Amy Oh yes.

Amy, still opening doors, laughs, while Frank holds up some whisky he has found.

And what's more, they never come off.

Frank Anyone?

Amy Not even at night.

Esme throws a caustic look towards Frank.

Esme It's all right. I've already warned Amy.

Frank What, that your nearest neighbour's a soak? I admit I have been drinking a lot. I know. But there you are. I know. (*He holds up his hands as if defending himself against an unseen critic.*)

Esme No one's worried!

Frank My life has been simply unspeakable. I'm allowed the consolations of drink.

Esme Mmm. (*She goes out to the kitchen.*)

Frank At least at the weekend. I drink more at the weekend. And today, after all, was a very special day. And you did wonderfully.

Esme (*off*) Thank you.

Frank (*to Amy*) Didn't she do wonderfully?

Esme reappears now, carrying two vases.

Esme Almost fifty-five and opening my very first fête. 'Our thanks to the people of Pangbourne . . .'

Amy Oh, God!

Esme happily sets about arranging her flowers. Frank is pouring three Scotches.

Esme I think now I've done it, I actually quite like it. Cutting ribbons. It's easier than acting. I think I might do it full time. 'Our thanks to the people of fill-in-at-random . . .'

Frank You wouldn't know the problems I had persuading her . . .

Esme I wasn't sure I was right for the role.

Amy has now aired the room and joins her mother, fetching scissors for the flowers' stems and handing them to her, one by one.

Frank But you pulled it off brilliantly.

Amy Perhaps just a touch of hauteur. The famous actress, among us, briefly, just briefly . . .

Esme Well, I had no intention of loitering.

Frank Among us and then she was gone! (*He hands Esme a whisky.*)

Esme Thank you. I was touched. I hadn't expected it. The fruit, the vegetables, all the little cakes. These people who turn out and sit at their stalls. All those ridiculous pickles. Is there anything which grows to which this is not the English response? 'If it's alive, then pickle it!' And those incredible wines!

Amy Did you try them?

42

Esme I did. That disgusting elderberry. And something – what was it? – parsnip cordial, or something like that.

Amy Rows and rows of jam. Jam coming out of their ears.

Esme Yes, I know. And you look at the flowers, the trestles, the tents and you think: just what is this? What *is* this occasion?

Frank What *is* it? What do you mean, what *is* it?

Esme I mean, you do wonder: is anyone fooled?

Esme has filled one vase and is deciding where to put it. Dominic has come downstairs. Now twenty-eight, he looks tidier, more prosperous, at ease in his fashionably casual clothes, and still wearing dark glasses. He is already speaking as he comes in with books in his hand.

Dominic Ah, there you are, Esme . . .

Esme Oh, Dominic . . . (*She laughs and accelerates across the room to avoid him.*) Oh, God . . .

Frank Fooled?

Dominic At last, now I've found you!

Esme Oh, Lord, I've been dreading it.

Dominic There's no reason we shouldn't do it right now.

Frank What do you mean, *fooled*?

Frank is standing in the middle of the room but they all ignore him.

Esme Can't you see I'm exhausted?

Amy What have you done with the children?

Dominic Don't worry. They're happy upstairs.

Amy looks tolerantly at him, then goes to the stairs to listen out for them.

Esme Dominic wants me to give him an interview, you know, for that programme of his.

Frank Oh yes. I may have seen it.

Dominic Today it's research. It's for filling in background.

Esme They were thrilled at the fête. They knew you were someone. They knew you were far more famous than me.

Dominic Oh, come on . . .

But Frank can't let go.

Frank I'm sorry, look, I know that I'm stupid . . .

Esme Frank isn't stupid.

Dominic They didn't think that.

Frank But I do have to point out: the village fête happens. It happens. By everyone's good efforts. People work to get it ready for most of the year . . .

Esme I'm sure they do.

Frank It means a great deal to us all.

Esme Yes, of course.

Amy returns and touches Dominic's arm.

Amy They seem to be quiet, it's OK.

Dominic What's all this about?

Frank So what are you asking when you say that you stand there and wonder if anyone's actually *fooled*?

Esme has gone to work on a second vase where Amy now joins her, cutting stems.

44

Esme Why surely, it happens. Frank, I know that it happens. I think we can agree it takes place. And, what's more, I admit, I found myself moved . . .

Frank There you are.

Esme But I'm also aware the whole thing is some sort of fiction . . .

Frank A fiction?

Esme Yes. Miss Marple! Thatched cottages! 'Congratulations to Mr Cox on the size of his enormous courgettes . . .' It's Heritage England. It's some sort of fantasy theme park, but don't tell me it actually still makes any sense.

Frank I don't see why not.

Esme suddenly raises her voice.

Esme Because this is a suburb!

Frank Oh, I see, now I get it . . .

Esme It's become a rich suburb, like any other, from where people like you, Frank, go to the City all day. You take the train to a place which enshrines your real values . . .

Frank Oh, really now, Esme. 'Real values'!

Esme And there you do your real work . . .

Frank So?

Esme So this place is not what it claims to be, this kind of organic community, rigged out with horses and jodhpurs and church choirs and such . . .

Dominic smiles to himself and sits down with his book at the side of the room.

Dominic Is this some sort of serious argument?

Esme I mean, why get an actress to open the proceedings unless the proceedings are kind of a fake?

Esme has dealt her coup de grâce, *but Frank is ready to counter-attack.*

Frank You know, she says something like this every evening. I come round every evening . . .

Amy You do?

Frank Well, nearly every evening.

Esme He comes pretty often.

Frank All right, but be fair, we have things to discuss.

Amy What things?

Frank Well, business.

Esme Frank comes to talk business, that's right.

Frank And always she's saying this isn't real country-side . . .

Esme It isn't.

Frank She says that life in the country is finished.

Esme It is! (*Underneath the banter, real feeling is beginning to show in Esme.*) Oh yes, of course, when Bernard was born . . . even by the time I first came . . . you could still look out over Berkshire. The glittering Thames. But now . . . it's basically Surbiton. But with the extra inconvenience that things are that much further apart. I walk a little bit *further* to Sainsbury's. I walk a little bit *further* to the garden centre. But otherwise, no. I'm living in Surbiton! And it's only the memory of what has now vanished that has me believing I still live where I did. (*She sits down and lights a cigarette.*)

Frank But that isn't fair. Everyone's here in the evening.

At weekends they make their life here. And they try to continue traditions which – let's face it – have lasted for hundreds of years.

Esme Yes, well, they go through the motions.

Frank is beginning to sound quite angry.

Frank And so what is the purpose? Why on earth do you think people persist with these rituals – these things that you say are just shams?

Esme pauses a moment. She is quiet.

Esme Because they know no alternative. Because they no longer know who they are.

Frank looks shocked at this answer. Esme stubs out her cigarette and makes to move.

Frank Well, I'm not sure I quite follow that one . . .

Esme Now who wants some supper?

Amy I'll do it. No, please let me, Ma.

Dominic Supper? Why sure . . .

Frank I'd say it's outrageous in fact.

Dominic But wouldn't it be better . . . I don't want to press you . . . but wouldn't it make better sense to do this thing first?

Esme Yes, of course. (*She stops at the door, looking round.*) I mean, yes, if you want to.

Amy Mum's been avoiding this moment all day.

Esme Nonsense. What makes you say that?

Dominic Because you'll do anything rather than sit down and talk! (*He has burst out, exasperated.*) We came down last night, I keep asking. Every time I look at you . . .

Esme Oh really!

Dominic You flit from the room.

Esme It's just not my *métier*!

Dominic Well, I wish you had said so.

Esme I did. I said so to Amy. The whole thing was Amy's idea.

Amy I just thought you'd enjoy it.

Esme Well, thank you. It's like going to the dentist for me. (*She leans down and kisses Amy.*)

Dominic Look . . .

Esme This ridiculous costume! I need five minutes to change. You must admit, I do look like a tree. It's simple. Just give me five minutes and then I promise I'm yours.

Esme has gone before anyone can protest. Dominic throws his book down and turns to Amy as if it is all her fault.

Amy All right . . .

Dominic I mean, this is it . . .

Amy All right!

Dominic I warned you. I did come down specially!

Frank She's impossible! She's like this every evening. She's truly impossible! (*He is grinning, proud of Esme.*)

Dominic It's obvious, Amy . . .

Amy Just be patient.

Dominic If she wanted to do it, she'd have done it by now.

Amy returns to the flowers to try and lie low, but Dominic is not going to let go.

And then, I can tell, it's just going to be *stories* . . .

Amy It's not.

Dominic She'll tell those awful theatrical stories of hers.

Amy No she won't.

Dominic How Perry dropped his props! How the set wobbled in Barnsley. How Deirdre can never remember her lines. If there's one thing that puts people off theatre, it's those meaningless stories they tell all the time.

Amy She's not going to tell stories. I've already warned her.

Dominic All right, then.

Amy I've said so. No stories!

Dominic looks at her doubtfully.

For Christ's sake, I've said so.

Dominic Well, all I can say is: she'd better not.

Frank is disturbed by Dominic's tone.

It's like she just doesn't realize. People are begging to appear on our show . . .

Amy I know . . .

Dominic I don't even write to them! Painters! Writers! Musicians! Truly. The A-list. I'm not boasting. I'm not. We don't even have to approach them. Really. You'd be astonished. We've reached the point where nearly always *they* approach *us*.

Amy Yes.

Dominic looks at his watch.

Dominic You know, I could still be in London. That's

what's so crazy. I could still be in London right now. There's this big media gathering . . .

Frank Oh really?

Dominic This conference. People coming in from all over the world . . .

Frank And I suppose you feel you should really be with them?

Dominic Believe it or not – again, I'm not being arrogant – but some people are flying in specifically because they know I'll be there!

Frank I see. (*He frowns at his drink, as if contemplating the problem.*)

Dominic It's a big thing. This country is changing. I work in independent production. It's a field where the British can well take a lead. And I have to wait while this – no offence – but this middle-aged actress decides when she's willing to favour me with ten minutes' chat. (*He knows he has gone too far.*)

Frank Well, I think . . .

Dominic Look, I'm sorry. That came out pretty ugly. If I'm angry, the truth is, I'm angry at myself. This is familiar behaviour from Esme. Amy, you know what I'm saying.

Amy just looks at him.

I think we've seen this before.

Frank looks between them, wanting to help.

Frank Perhaps . . . I don't know . . . perhaps you could call them.

Dominic Call who?

Frank These big media people of yours.

50

Dominic Call to say what? That I'm stuck in the country? That I have no idea when I'll get back?

Amy is shaking with anger, but it comes out low, suppressed.

Amy Dominic, I never ask you for anything. Just do me this favour, all right?

Esme returns in slacks, carrying a couple of plates of hors d'oeuvres.

Esme All right, here I am, now I'm ready for your questions.

Dominic Good.

Esme Salami? Go ahead . . .

Dominic Thank you.

Esme Ask any questions you like.

Dominic I was thinking perhaps we might do this in private.

Esme Oh, do you think so? I was hoping that everyone might want to join in.

Frank Not me.

Esme Dominic's planning this programme. We all sit under spotlights. In a studio. Debating.

Frank And what is the subject to be?

Esme looks sweetly at Dominic.

Esme No, really. It's your idea. Tell him.

Dominic We're discussing the question of whether the theatre is dead.

There is a slightly sticky moment.

Amy Dead?

Frank Oh, I see.

Dominic I told you that, Amy.

Amy I didn't realize it was quite as dramatic as that.

Dominic Well, we might as well face it. It is a real question. To people of my generation at least. In the old days it seemed like theatre was really exciting. In those days, it still had something to say . . .

Esme offers the salami to Amy, who takes the chance to put her hand on Esme's arm.

Esme Amy?

Dominic But now . . . I don't know, we're all watching video. I believe human beings have changed. They've evolved. They have different priorities.

Frank My goodness.

Dominic The image is much more important. The image has taken the place of the word.

Frank nods and tries to look intelligent.

Frank Uh-huh.

Dominic You know, you go to the theatre. A character comes in the door. You think, oh my God! He's going to cross the room. Jump-cut, for Christ's sake, just jump-cut! And then next thing – oh, Christ, you just know it! The bastard is going to sit down and *talk*. (*He shakes his head pityingly.*) And it's so slow. They do it slowly. And the way they act! It's so old-fashioned. In these big barns and they all have to shout. Why don't we admit it? It's been superseded. It had its moment, but its moment has gone.

Amy looks nervously across at her mother, but Esme is not remotely concerned.

Of course, I defer to you, Esme . . .

Esme Thank you . . .

Dominic You understand it all much better than me. But who does theatre reach? Who is it talking to? Obvious. To me, it's just wank time.

Esme I see. Well, it's good that at least you've not made up your mind . . .

Dominic Look . . .

Esme No, really, that famed objectivity. He's open-minded . . .

Amy (*smiles*) Yes . . .

Esme Wouldn't you say? Dominic has no agenda or anything . . .

Dominic All right, very funny . . .

Esme There's no question of you boys having to work to a script! (*She seems oddly cheered as she moves round with the plates.*) Have you noticed? It's always the death of the theatre. The death of the novel. The death of poetry. The death of whatever they fancy this week. Except there's one thing it's never the death of. Somehow it's never the death of *themselves*.

Dominic Esme . . .

Esme The death of television! The death of the journalist! I can't think why, but we never get those. It's off to the scaffold with everyone except for the journalists!

Amy It's true.

Esme Now I wonder why can that be?

Esme moves away laughing as Amy begins to clear the table for supper.

Amy It's pointless arguing with Esme. As she says, she doesn't do argument.

Esme I don't.

Amy She only does instincts. The worst thing, I tell you . . .

Esme My instincts are usually right!

Amy Usually, Ma! Usually!

The two women laugh together, happy.

Esme Though I must say it's kind of unfortunate, Dominic happening to ask me right now . . .

Amy Why?

Esme I've been thinking about giving up acting.

Amy Oh yeah? Really? I wonder where I've heard that before . . .

Esme lights a cigarette blithely.

Esme I'm thinking of leaving the field free for Deirdre. She gave an interview – did you see it?

Amy No . . .

Esme The usual rubbish. The cover of *Radio Times*. She claims she's never been interested in sex. 'It bores me,' she says. I thought, in that case, I know for a certainty, you've been bored stiff for most of your life!

But Amy is frowning now.

Amy But Mum . . .

Esme What? Am I serious? Is that what you're waiting to ask?

Amy Yes.

Esme I do have a problem.

Frank Oh really!

Esme How can I say I'm an actress when the point is I no longer act?

Frank That isn't true. (*He has given Esme a second drink.*)

Esme In my head I'm an actress. But what have I actually done? A radio broadcast from Birmingham. A voice-over. For a green disinfectant, in fact. I played a germ. And meanwhile it's . . . what? Three years? No, four since I actually appeared in a play . . .

Frank Well . . .

Esme So you might say it's hardly the moment for me to hold forth on your programme. 'Why I believe in the drama' and such!

But Dominic is beginning to get excited.

Dominic No. On the contrary, it seems to me perfect. 'There are no parts for women,' I've heard you say that . . .

Esme Oh . . .

Dominic Well, now here's your chance to say it in public . . .

Esme Yes, maybe that's what's putting me off.

Dominic Why?

Esme A natural diffidence. 'There are no parts for women.' Another way of putting it: 'I'm out of work!'

She shares the absurdity of it with Frank, but Dominic persists, vehement.

Frank No, you're right.

Dominic Exactly! No women – that's part of what's wrong with the theatre. It's one of the reasons why I never go.

Amy Dominic, you are so full of shit. You never go because you never go anywhere where you're meant to turn off your mobile . . .

Dominic Now, Amy, that is just stupid . . .

Amy And also where you have to shut up and sit still. (*She has suddenly come to life.*)

Dominic Look . . .

Amy No, I finally got him to go the opera. On comes this dying diva. All round the death-bed. *La Traviata*. Act Four. She opens her mouth. Beep beep from Dominic's pocket!

Dominic All right, but at least it rang a high C.

Amy Oh, sure. A call from America! From someone to say they'd call back later on. Which is all anyone seems to say on these things. 'I'm calling to let you know I'll be calling you later . . .'

Dominic Amy hates them.

Amy It's the only way the children know he exists.

Esme Really?

Amy Chloe did a drawing of her father. She had him with a phone to each ear!

Dominic Chloe exaggerates. Chloe is a child who exaggerates.

Amy No, she's not. The tragedy is, she draws what she sees . . .

Esme has sat down, quietly watching this argument develop between them.

Every evening the phone rings at seven. Then again at eight. Then at nine. It's always Dominic. 'Oh, I'm held up at work.'

56

Dominic Well, I am!

Amy Then it's midnight. I'm sleeping. Always in a bed of wet nappies, of course. 'Oh, Amy, can't speak.' If you can't speak why call me? Why call me? 'I'm with this producer. Don't worry, I shan't be long now . . .'

Dominic is suddenly quiet, lethal.

Dominic Well, what do you want? Do you want I don't call you?

Amy No.

Dominic Do you want I never call you at all?

There is a moment. They have fallen into a real, disastrous row. Amy turns away.

Amy Oh please, let's leave it. Just leave it.

Esme watches from the side, quite still.

I want to ask Mum how she'd manage to live.

Esme Me?

Amy Yes.

Esme I suppose, on my income. Remember, I always have Frank.

Frank I control her portfolio.

Esme Frank is my saviour. He allows me to ignore all that nonsense. I never read any of that stuff myself.

Frank She doesn't!

Esme I don't even take in the figures . . .

Frank It's true. They just pass before her eyes!

Esme I don't care. As long as there's food in the larder . . . I know! I'm just lucky that Frank came along.

She throws a warm glance to Frank, who basks in her approval. Amy watches, trying to understand what is going on.

Frank And I must say, you know, since my wife died, I admit, my evenings had been fairly bleak. With no Sarah. So to come round and talk about Esme's investments . . .

Esme Drink whisky.

Frank That too. For me, it's been very healing. It has. I owe Esme everything. Yes, in her quiet way, she's nursed me back to good mental health.

Frank seems almost overwhelmed. Amy is tentative, a little confused.

Amy And you think she could manage . . . she could get by financially?

Frank Why, yes. Not to live like John Paul Getty, of course. But surviving. Managing to live with some sort of dignity.

Esme And God knows dignity's not nothing these days.

Amy But what would you *do*?

Esme Oh, there's far too much talk about 'doing'. If I gave up, then I'd just have to get on and 'be'.

She is half-satirical. But Amy is dismayed.

Amy Well, I'm just stunned.

Esme Why?

Amy It seems so extraordinary. Dominic.

Dominic Hmm?

Amy What do you think?

Dominic Oh. I've always thought the theatre was boring. So I quite see why you want to get out.

Esme is amused by this, but Amy is not.

Amy That's not quite what she was saying.

Dominic No. She said something like it.

Esme Oh, Dominic! Making mischief again!

Dominic Is that what I do?

Esme A professional passer of judgements! (*She makes a little mock swipe with her hand at Frank.*) Frank, you're not really saying you've missed this little programme of his.

Frank Well . . .

Esme Dominic's our cultural arbiter. He exists to tells us what's good.

Dominic Not at all.

Esme He informs the public what they should be seeing.

Dominic On the contrary! 'Should' isn't in it. It's to get rid of 'should' that the programme exists.

Frank 'Should'?

Dominic Yes, we all know that art is encrusted in snob-bery. People feel frightened. The arts establishment tries to make them feel cowed.

Frank I see.

Dominic So we say to them: 'Don't be bullied. Just follow your own instincts. Don't let anyone dictate to you. Make up your own minds.'

Esme is eager to join in.

Esme At the end . . .

Dominic Yes . . .

Esme They have a small item.

Dominic Very brief.

Esme What's it called?

Amy It's called *Not Up to Snuff*.

Esme That's right. Where they kindly bring the public up to date on art which they feel has been over-praised.

Dominic is beginning to feel goaded.

Dominic Why not? I don't apologize.

Esme There's a little animated figure . . .

Dominic This drawing . . .

Esme This little cartoon bloke in a cap, and he takes the work they discuss. Then he throws it . . .

Frank Oh yes, now I remember. I've seen it!

Esme He throws it into a bathroom.

Dominic Splash!

Esme And you then hear the sound of a loo being flushed. It's wit. (*She smiles.*)

Dominic All right, but why do we do it? Because there's so much hype, there's so much palaver, there's so many people claiming to be artists these days.

Esme Is that right?

Dominic So why not invent some sort of decent corrective, in which you say: 'Hold on, let's just be serious. Is this thing as good as everyone makes out?'

Esme watches from the side, glass in hand, pleased with the bonfire she's lit.

Frank Interesting.

Dominic Like a book . . . you buy a book. What is it? Twelve pounds? Thirteen? We're there to say: now let's just be careful. Is this really all it's cracked up to be?

Esme Ah, you're performing a public duty, you mean? (*She moves round the room with her drink.*) Ah, yes. Like a hangman. Reluctant, but responsible. 'It's a dirty job but it's got to be done.' Is that it? You're – what? – *public-spirited*? But that doesn't quite explain the relish you show.

Dominic What relish?

Esme When something is awful.

Dominic I say so.

Esme Yes.

Dominic What's wrong with that?

Esme Oh, nothing. Just that glint round the eyes. That smile. 'Oh, God be praised, I've got a real stinker. What happiness! Now I can really rip into this . . .'

Dominic is beginning to get angry.

Dominic Look . . . what . . . so what are you saying? Do you think I've some kind of personal axe to grind?

Esme Oh, seriously now, Dominic, come on!

Dominic *What?*

Esme has turned away laughing.

Esme It's not for me to say, but years ago – remember? – when I first met you – with Amy – you wanted to make your own films.

Dominic Well, I do!

Esme I mean real films! Not people wittering about other peoples' work. I mean, actual new-minted stories.

Showing people. In the grip of real passions.

But Dominic is already shaking his head.

Dominic Oh, that's simply old-fashioned. It really is nonsense! I don't accept that distinction at all.

Esme No?

Dominic Of course not. That whole old-fashioned notion! Criticism can be just as creative as making up *stories*, you know. Sometimes more so. Seeing things clearly, placing them, giving them context: that work is just as important as art.

Esme You think so? (*She grins conspiratorially at Amy.*)

Dominic Oh, I suppose you think it's all down to jealousy. Of course! Isn't that what actors and writers all say? I must somehow be jealous. The perpetual excuse! Critics only hate you because they've not had the guts to make crappy British features or churn out turgid middle-class novels themselves.

Esme just smiles, as if his tone proved her case.

Esme Well . . .

Dominic I suppose you think critics are all fuelled by jealousy?

Esme Not all of them, no.

Dominic But you think that I am?

Esme looks at him a moment, serious.

Esme I think you're aware of your power.

Dominic I most certainly hope so. Because the point is, I try to use it for good. (*He has, in his view, won the argument.*) And the result is, the programme's almost absurdly successful . . .

Esme I know that.

Dominic Its ratings are way beyond what anyone hoped. Because it actually puts itself – unlike all the others – on the side of the consumer . . .

Esme The consumer?

Dominic Yes. By which I mean ordinary people like me . . .

Esme Oh . . .

Dominic And this whole – you know – arty flim-flammery, this whole elitist nonsense of 'bloody-well-like-this' and 'we-know-what's-what' – I tell you, that attitude's over. It's finished.

Esme Well, thank God at least we're clear about that.

Dominic looks at her warily.

It is the most wonderful casting. The country's most famous, most influential programme which lays down the law on the arts. And it's run by a man who seems to have only one small disadvantage. What is it? Remind me. Oh yes, I remember. (*She suddenly looks across the room at him with real savagery.*) It turns out he doesn't like art!

She has lit the blue touch paper but, before Dominic can react, Evelyn comes into the room. She is eighty-four. She is still physically firm, in one of her tartan skirts and pullovers. But, when Esme gets up to usher her to her favoured chair, you see that she is being treated differently.

Ah, Evelyn. All right?

Evelyn I thought I heard voices.

Esme You did.

Evelyn There are people here.

63

Esme Yes, that's right. This is Dominic.

Evelyn Dominic?

Dominic Evelyn.

Esme You remember? And Amy.

Amy Grandma.

Evelyn Yes, I remember. And you? Who are you?

Esme I'm your daughter-in-law. I'm Esme.

Evelyn And Bernard? Where's Bernard?

Esme I'm afraid to say Bernard's not here.

Evelyn Not here?

Esme No. Bernard is dead.

Evelyn Dead?

Esme Do me a favour, Frank. Can you just get her a drink?

Evelyn has sat down, very confused now. Dominic is restless wanting to interrupt.

Dominic Look . . .

Evelyn He's dead and nobody told me?

Esme Nonsense. We told you, it's just you forget.

Evelyn How could you not tell me?

She is beginning to cry. Esme is signalling urgently to Frank.

Esme More. More. Just keep pouring.

Amy Are you sure that it's good for her?

Evelyn You didn't even tell me. How could you?

Esme I live with her, remember?

Evelyn Why did nobody tell me?

Esme ignores Evelyn's crying.

Dominic I'm sorry, I'm aware that somehow you all think it's funny . . .

Amy Oh, God, now that *is* the children this time . . .

Amy goes to the hall, as Dominic goes on.

Dominic There's some sort of hidden agreement in play . . .

Frank holds up a huge measure of Scotch.

Esme Yes, that's fine.

Dominic You think you can all just dump on my programme . . .

Esme (*taking it*) Thank you . . .

Dominic 'Oh, it's all just this trivial rubbish on telly. So it doesn't matter, we can say what we like . . .'

Esme Oh, really now, Dominic . . .

Dominic Whereas – please! – just imagine the horror if I decided that this was a two-way privilege. Oh, if I decided to tell the truth about you!

Frank looks puzzled, but Esme turns, at last giving Dominic her whole attention.

Frank What truth?

Esme Dominic, you're highly successful. You've no reason to worry. You now have the power you craved.

Dominic But of course in your view that's vulgar and nasty . . .

Esme I haven't said anything!

Dominic Because you think it's wrong to want to get on! It's somehow distasteful. Power is something it's vulgar to want. Or at least to admit to wanting. In the terms that you live in, we all know, I'm faintly embarrassing.

Amy is returning through the hall and Dominic is prompted by the sound of her.

The family has someone who does things of which they don't approve!

Evelyn It's good. Can I have some more?

Esme No, not now.

Amy is at the door, unaware of what has gone on.

Amy Dominic, you did say you'd bath them.

Dominic I will bath them.

Amy Well, when?

There is a new determination in Dominic's eye.

Dominic I will do it. I will bath them just as I promised. And then – I'm sorry – but I'm going to take them back home.

Amy What?

Dominic Yes. I'm just tired of this snobbery . . .

Amy What snobbery?

Esme Oh really!

Frank Now steady on, old chap . . .

Dominic This unspoken assumption. You know what I'm saying. Always! This permanent leer of good taste! Whenever I come here, I walk into this household . . .

Amy Oh . . .

66

Dominic I just have to take one look at the walls. And suddenly I'm back in short trousers. I feel like I'm back to being fifteen years old.

Amy looks, but Esme is not reacting.

And you two go into a huddle. The two of you. Smiling and giggling like schoolgirls in each others' ears. And at once I'm no better than some sort of dustman or servant.

Amy Dominic, I think you exaggerate.

Evelyn has been peering at Dominic.

Evelyn Is that man Bernard?

Esme I think we can safely say that he's not.

Dominic is expressing years of grievance and he's not going to let go.

Dominic And I do understand. Yes, of course, you resent me. You're right. I work in a medium on which you look down. You pretend it's not good. But in fact that's not your real reason. You really don't like it because television brings you bad news. Because actually, in some crude way, it does belong to the people . . .

Esme Oh, Dominic, 'the people'! (*She laughs out loud, mocking him.*) What do you know about 'the people' indeed?

Dominic Yes, and the fact is, you don't bloody like it because it reflects all the real feelings they have. Yes, the truth is: you fear it. Because in its awful, gaudy vitality, television reminds you of what people think. And when you hear their opinions, when you see the evidence of their real taste, then it's pitifully obvious: the sheer downright irrelevance of this self-enclosed arty little world that you've made.

Esme Oh . . .

Dominic People love things which you think are vulgar. They've no time for the stuff which you think so great! (*He smiles, anticipating his own joke.*) Forgive me, but a lot of people love Deirdre Keane. They think she's a very fine actress.

Esme Dominic, now I know you're not serious. There's no one in the world who really thinks that.

Amy Look, Dominic . . .

Dominic What?

Amy Can't you just leave it?

Dominic Why should I?

Amy Not everything is directed at you. You always do this. It's one of those stupid, meaningless arguments . . .

Dominic You're wrong. In this case, it happens to mean a great deal.

Amy Dominic . . .

Dominic I'm swamped in this bloody English gentility! You yourself said it. It's typical. Opening this absurd bloody fête! But the question is, will that stop you doing it? Oh no, not you. You want it both ways. Both to do it and mock it.

Amy Dominic . . .

Dominic The English attitude to their own institutions: defend them to strangers but laugh at them yourselves! The privilege of not seeming to take anything seriously. But still making sure that nothing is changed!

Esme is quiet. He knows he has hit home.

If you don't want to do the programme, then say so! Instead of just trying to get me provoked.

Amy She's not trying. I'd say she's succeeding.

Dominic Yes. As it happens she is. (*He looks unforgivingly at Amy.*) Because I've always thought this.
Whenever we've visited, I've had the same thought. She is permitted to look down on how I make my living. But I'm not permitted to look down on hers.

There is a depth of feeling now which silences the others. Frank tries to help.

Frank I'm sorry, I've been standing here. But I haven't heard anything – not one single syllable – to cause you such desperate offence. All right, you were arguing about culture. I know nothing about culture. I'm the first to admit. The last film I saw was *Doctor Zhivago*. In my opinion, it was pretty good. But even if someone came along and said, no, you're wrong, it was bollocks, it hardly seems to me important. It's not worth risking a friendship for that.

Dominic But we're not. That's not the argument. We're not talking about art. Isn't that right? No, we're discussing something quite different.

Frank What's that?

Neither Esme nor Dominic want to answer.

What are you discussing?

Dominic Whether I deserve her daughter or not.

Evelyn Her daughter?

Amy makes to intervene, but Dominic overrides her.

Amy Dominic . . .

Dominic You know, she once told me Amy was pregnant. She told me before Amy herself. Yes. You remember that evening? When your mother blurted it out? (*He looks now at Amy.*) I wonder, do you know why she did that?

69

Did you believe her when she said it just sort of slipped out? 'Just sort of *slipped out*'? No, I don't think so. She said it in the hope I might then go away. (*He waits, giving Esme a chance to deny it.*) She's never come to terms with the fact Amy loves me. She thinks that Amy is wrong to share her life on my terms.

Amy She's never said that.

Dominic Hasn't she? She thinks you shouldn't have taken me. She hates the arrangement we made.

Amy Please.

Dominic It was clear. I am free to get on with my work. Well, it's true. We did agree that. Didn't we? Esme disapproved.

Esme's face is set like a mask.

You see, she can't answer. She won't. That's Esme. To her credit, she'll never say the kind thing. But why don't we stop this dancing round each other's feelings? Why don't I simply stop coming down?

Esme Fine.

Amy Mum . . .

Dominic I didn't want you on the programme.

Esme No. No, I can see that.

Dominic The whole thing was Amy's idea.

Esme Yes.

Dominic Because . . . well, we know Amy . . . it's Amy's view that everyone should try to get on. (*There is a moment's silence.*) Well, I say, no actually, let's really not bother. The mistake is to try and be kind. Like employing actresses to talk about theatre for no other reason but they're down on their luck.

Amy looks down, embarrassed by this now.

I didn't think it was sensible. I didn't want my girlfriend's mother, you see. Because I knew I'd be having her for the wrong reasons . . .

Esme Yes.

Dominic And things always go wrong when they're done in bad faith. (*He moves towards the door.*) It's up to you, Amy. I can take the children or not. Please. Either stay the weekend with your mother. Or else why not come back with me?

He goes out and up the stairs. We hear him calling to the children. Evelyn has fallen asleep. Amy takes a step towards Esme, who is giving nothing away.

Amy I wonder . . . do you think you could go and see if he'll talk to you?

Esme looks at her as if she doesn't understand the question.

Mum, I do know it isn't your fault. But if you . . . I don't know . . . if you just went up and talked to him . . .

Frank You could at least talk to him, Esme.

Esme Oh, so you think that as well? (*She walks across the room. She lights a cigarette.*) What, I'm meant to apologize?

Amy No.

Esme I'm meant to pretend I've done something wrong? (*She shrugs slightly.*) He's right. There are people who are simply not meant to get on. Amy, you do it from kindness. I know that. I know it's your view that love conquers all. But it doesn't. Or at least, that's what I've learned.

At once from upstairs the sound of Dominic calling down.

Dominic (*off*) Are you coming, Amy? Are we taking the children? They're ready. They can go back.

Amy (*calls*) Just give me a minute. (*She looks all the time at Esme. Calls*) I just need a minute to make up my mind.

Dominic (*off*) We're going.

Amy takes a step towards Esme.

Esme Come on, it's not so dramatic, it's not so disastrous as that. We'll see each other. I'll see the children.

Amy You've never understood. You know that I love him. You never see the man who I love.

Esme No. And if I was going to, I fear the moment has passed. Now I'm getting supper.

She has suddenly moved dismissively, but Amy is infuriated by her answer.

Dominic (*off*) Amy!

Amy Why do you say that? You still can't forgive me. You can't forgive the choice that I made.

Esme It was wrong.

Amy It isn't your business. And the reason you make it your business is because you have no life of your own!

Dominic (*off*) Amy! Let's go!

Amy turns and goes out. Esme is suddenly stilled by what Amy has said. She stands at the table where she had been headed.

Amy (*off*) Are you ready?

Dominic (*off*) Yes. I've got all your things. Come on, we're going. Just give me a hand.

There is the sound of them on the stairs. Then it goes quiet.

Esme Frank, I wonder, perhaps now this evening . . .

Frank Of course. Tomorrow I'll give you a call.

Esme Would you? I'd like that.

Frank nods and moves out through the veranda, patting his pockets as he goes.

Frank Are you all right, Esme?

Esme I promise, I'm fine.

Frank goes out. It is nearly dark outside. Esme moves to clear up the glasses and plates. From outside the sound of the children and the adults. Then the door slamming and the car driving away. As Esme collects the last plate, Evelyn wakes.

Evelyn Where's Bernard? Somebody tell me. Where's Bernard?

Esme Evelyn, I've told you. Bernard is dead.

Evelyn Yes. (*There is a short pause.*) And so tell me one more thing. Where's Bernard?

Esme goes into the veranda. She sets down a chair where she can sit with her back to us and stare at the night sky. Then after a while she answers.

Esme Bernard's not here. Bernard is dead.

INTERVAL

73

Act Three

The same. It is eight years later. A summer night in 1993.
It is very dark. A single lamp burns at the table, throwing
big shadows all over the room. Frank is sitting in shirt-
sleeves and corduroys, working alone. The table is piled
up with books and documents. He has glasses on and has
been working for many hours. His customary bottle of
whisky is beside him. At some distance from him, Evelyn
is asleep in a wheelchair. She is ninety-two. She is very
thin with an astonishingly pale face and a shock of white
hair. She sleeps with her mouth open.

After a few moments, Frank looks up at the sound of
someone moving outside. Amy appears through the veranda
entrance. Now in her late thirties, she looks thinner than
ever, and quite aged, almost gaunt. She comes quickly into
the room, like a refugee, not realizing there is anyone there.

Amy My god, you surprised me.

Frank I'm sorry.

Amy The veranda was open. (*There is a moment's*
unease.) I didn't know you'd be here. (*She hesitates, then*
kisses him, just brushing his cheek.) Frank.

Frank Hello, Amy. Are you looking for your mother?

Amy Well, yes. Is she always this late?

Frank No. But today there's a big operation . . .

Amy Oh, right.

Frank She's been building up to it all week. And they can
be quite tricky.

Amy nods, understanding.

I wish she would learn to drive herself back.

Amy looks at him a moment.

Amy And you?

Frank Me?

Amy Are you actually living here?

Frank Oh . . .

Amy Are you living here now?

Frank Do I really live here? I think you'd have to ask Esme. And will you please let me know what she says?

Amy puts her car keys down on the table.

Amy And do you bring her supper?

Frank Oh, well, meals can be quite chaotic.

Amy Does she still get her stuff from the pub?

Frank Surely you noticed . . .

Amy No, I didn't see anything . . .

Frank No pub any more.

Amy Really?

Frank is trying to put her at ease.

Frank They've made it a wine bar. Everything's changed. You can only get wind-dried yak meat. Native Berkshire dishes like that. Served with alfalfa sprout salad.

Amy Good gracious.

Frank Oh, Lord, yes. All washed down with Aqua Libra on draught.

Amy has begun to move round the room, looking at the walls.

Amy And how's Mum?

Frank Bearing up. Considering. I've been trying to persuade her to move out of here . . .

Amy Ah.

Frank After what's happened. It's frankly too large. She could even live in London. Why not? But you know your mother.

Amy Stubborn.

Frank Yes.

Amy I was expecting the walls to be stripped.

Frank Not yet.

Amy Has she sold any paintings?

Frank I'm not even sure she would if she could. (*He grimaces slightly.*) Your father isn't collected. Except by people who loved and remember the man. And now even they are all turning seventy.

Amy Yes. I suppose.

Frank Bernard's almost completely forgotten. Except by one or two students. One of them came here, said, 'I'm not really interested, if you want to know the truth. But Bernard Thomas is perfect for a thesis. He's just the right degree of obscure.'

He smiles wryly, but Amy doesn't respond.

I wonder . . . can I get you anything?

Amy shakes her head.

Did your mother know you'd be here?

Amy No.

Frank I must say . . . she didn't mention it . . .

Amy We haven't spoken for a while.

Frank waits a moment.

Frank It's funny. In some way she's carefree. After such a disaster. I know it's perverse. But in some way it's made her much happier.

Amy Yes, I can see that.

Frank A burden's been lifted.

Amy frowns at him, concentrating now.

Amy You've been with her a lot?

Frank Well, I do have a pair of pyjamas. There's a pair I keep in this house.

Amy But where are they?

Frank Oh, sadly they're in the guest room. But, remember, the guest room is not far from Esme's.

Amy I see.

Frank She wakes in the night, to be honest. Her dreams are very intense. I sit by the bed till she sleeps.

Amy She's always alone?

Frank does not answer.

Frank I think you know what I feel for her, Amy. I can't help it, I've felt the same way for years. Perhaps even before my wife died. People say to me, 'You're crazy, you can't go on doing this. You've waited such a long time.' I say, 'And I'll wait longer.'

Amy Yes. (*She looks beyond him to Evelyn.*) And Evelyn?

Frank Oh, Evelyn. Does she hear? She no longer speaks. The fretting is over.

Amy passes a hand right in front of Evelyn's face but there is no reaction.

You can never tell. Has she accepted her fate?

Esme appears, stopping at once at the sight of Amy. Now in her early sixties, she is carrying a bundle of envelopes.

Esme Well, Amy, good gracious.

She has spoken quietly, and Amy turns in surprise.

Amy Mum. I didn't hear you.

Esme Oh no? I'm afraid I did take a taxi. I know I shouldn't, but I thought what the hell? Frank doesn't like it.

Neither of the women knows what to do. They stand a moment, lost.

Amy Are you all right?

Esme Yes. I'm exhausted. It's been a tough day. Why haven't you called me?

Amy Oh . . .

Esme makes a useless gesture with her hand, and the dam bursts. She moves and embraces Amy, weeping.

Esme Oh, my God, Amy. Amy, how I've missed you, my darling . . .

Amy I know.

Esme It's been so awful. No, really . . .

Amy Oh, Mum . . .

Esme is crying, overwhelmed and running her hands through Amy's hair.

Esme Really, no really, I'm fine . . .

Amy Oh, Mother . . .

Esme is deliberately pulling herself away to try and recover from her outburst.

Esme Honestly it's . . . oh, it's . . . oh, it's so silly, forgive me, I can't even speak.

Amy Don't worry. (*She holds her mother's head in her hands a moment and looks into her eyes.*) Don't worry!

Esme It's also . . .

Amy Go on.

Esme What does it matter? You're here. (*Impulsively, she hugs her daughter again.*)

Amy It's all right. Go on, say . . .

Esme Oh, Lord, I know I sound selfish . . .

Amy You don't . . .

Esme But the fact is, the truth is: I have had one hell of a day.

They both laugh at the absurdity, and Esme moves away to recover from the emotion.

Amy Well, I'm sure.

Esme I can't tell you, we had this patient . . .

Amy What patient?

Esme Oh, you know . . .

Frank Do you want a drink?

Esme waves a hand in dismissal.

Esme An old man of seventy. It was awful. He needed a new aorta.

Amy An aorta?

Esme Yes. There's no question, if we hadn't done it, he would have died.

Amy Well . . .

Frank Sit down.

Esme You've probably heard, there's this new operation . . .

Amy No. No, of course not. How could I have heard?

Esme You take a valve from a pig . . .

Amy A pig?

Esme You extract it, you keep it in ice. You take this little rounded ring of pig's muscle . . .

Frank It's true.

Esme And you sew it into the heart of the patient, it serves to replace the patient's own valve . . .

Amy I see.

Esme No, really it's almost standard procedure. But the point is, you're working very intensely – well, you can imagine – you're at this very high pitch . . .

Amy Sure.

Esme There's blood everywhere, great thick pools of it . . .

Amy My God!

Esme Crimson! Then there's the lasers, the burning . . . the flesh being cut . . . (*She shakes her head.*) I turn round, I'm passing the scalpel, I look down at this hand next to mine. This little nurse has actually got a ring on her finger. And what's more she's wearing this awful clunky paste bangle . . .

Frank looks nervously at Amy, as if fearing where this story is going.

I simply think: no, I cannot believe this. I'm sorry. No, really!

Frank I can imagine . . .

Esme And the fact is . . . . (*She pauses for a moment.*) Well, I'm afraid I just go.

Amy Go?

Esme Yes, what I mean is, I started to shout at her. I was shouting! Amy, I do know it's wrong. But it's so unhygienic. What, I'm meant to say nothing?

Frank This isn't the first time . . .

Esme I say, 'What the hell's going on?'

Frank smiles uneasily at Amy.

Frank What does she say?

Esme I say, 'This is serious.' This nurse, she's just so weedy, she's like this weedy little thing. I've never even seen her before. I say, 'For Christ's sake, it's a major operation. The cameras see everything.' She just stands there. She looks at me like I'm going mad.

Frank Well, I'm sure.

Esme So now the whole studio's stopping. The director – oh, he's coming down from on high! This little idiot starts sulking. She says, 'Oh, come on, it's only TV.' (*She pauses, furious.*) Well . . .

Frank My God!

Esme No, I'm sorry, but to me that's unforgivable. You can say anything but you must never say that.

Frank smiles again at Amy.

Frank This has happened before.

Esme 'If we do it, we make it authentic, or else let's not do it at all . . .' Well, it's true! That's the whole principle. Do it properly! You have to ask yourself, 'Is it real or is it not?'

Amy frowns, not able to answer.

Anyway, by now – oh, bloody chaos! The surgeon's dropped the scalpel in this awful prop pool of blood. The patient's sitting up on the table, he says, 'I'm sorry to ask this, but do I get a new aorta or not?'

Frank That's funny.

Esme People are gathering. They're saying, 'Look, we know you've been under great strain.' I'm screaming, 'It's not me, for Christ's sake. Why are you getting at me? It's that little tart with her sugar daddy's jewellery, she's the one who's destroying the show . . .' (*She has suddenly become quite vicious.*)

Frank (*to Amy*) What about you? Will you have a drink?

Esme Apart from anything, just think of my character . . .

Frank Nurse Banstead . . .

Esme From her point of view – well, think of it, you've seen the show . . .

Amy looks non-committal.

It's obvious. She's called a disciplinarian. You could say. Or you could say she's just one tough bloody bitch.

Frank Oh, she is!

Esme Whichever. Do you really think she'd permit it? It's inconceivable! It's just unprofessional. I'm sorry, forget it, but that's what I think.

Frank seems nervous of his next question.

Frank But . . .

Esme But what?

Frank You did resume shooting?

Esme What? Well, after an hour or two, sure. We had to get a new valve. (*She looks angrily at Frank.*) Oh, Frank, please, I do know what you're asking. I'm not stupid! The only thing that concerns him . . .

Frank Well . . .

Esme Will I get thrown off the show?

Amy is frowning, not really understanding what's going on between them.

With Frank it's all about money, there's nothing but money. Every night he tells me 'You must hold on to this job . . .'

Frank Well, you must!

Esme 'For your own sake,' he says, 'just keep your head down . . .' That's Frank! Anything rather than let me speak out!

Frank turns to Amy silently to ask what choice he has.

And I say, 'What? I'm just meant to endure these conditions? When the theatre is filthy? When peoples' lives are at risk?'

Frank Esme . . .

Esme I'm meant to say nothing? When basic medical

procedure is flouted in front of my eyes? I'm sorry, I don't care, I'm not going to do it. I do have a conscience! There are times when it's simply too much.

Frank Of course.

Esme has picked up the envelopes she has earlier put down on the table.

Esme He never lets me forget the white envelopes . . . (*She makes a fist of them in her hand.*) Oh, I'm not opening them. I'm going to talk to my daughter instead.

Frank Do you want me to do it?

Esme No. They're my bloody envelopes. Thank you. I'll open these bastards myself.

Frank stands rebuked.

It's the post . . . the post is so frightening. I try to leave it until I get back. So that way . . .

Frank It makes no difference.

Esme I don't go to work in the morning . . .

Amy I can imagine . . .

Esme Simply not able to think.

Frank is enjoying this.

Frank She used to put them under the cushions . . .

Esme Oh really!

Frank It's true. I'd go round in the day, just feeling all the cracks in sofas to see if I'd come across more!

Esme All right, but it isn't actually as stupid as you think it is. You get the same letters again and again. So for God's sake . . . (*She suddenly gives up.*) Oh, stuff it! I actually don't want to discuss it. Not tonight. Can we please not discuss it? I haven't seen Amy for months.

Amy No.

Frank looks between them.

Frank Perhaps I should go. I'll make you both cocoa. Esme always has a cup before bed.

Esme That's great. Yes, will you? (*She waves a hand ironically.*) My domestic servant.

Frank If it was meant as a joke, then perhaps I would laugh. (*He goes out, closing the door.*)

Esme Oh really!

Amy He's funny. He is so devoted.

Esme Yes. I'm afraid he is desperate to marry me though. What's worse, it's getting more urgent. If I don't do it, he says he's going to give up.

Amy But he just told me the opposite . . .

Esme Did he?

Amy He told me he'd wait for you.

Esme Oh, I wish it were true. In fact there's a deadline. Yes, by Christmas.

Amy And what will you do?

Esme Oh, Christmas! I can't even see beyond Wednesday. I don't know. One day I'm afraid I may have to give in. I'll get into his Ford Granada. Drive cross-country. Do it in some county town with nobody there. Spend the honeymoon in one of those phoney ivy-clad riverside hotels. (*She gets a cigarette, suddenly exasperated.*) How did it happen? I never foresaw this! Never!

Amy is unimpressed by the theatricality of her complaint.

Amy Oh, come on, it isn't that bad.

Esme Isn't it?

Amy Of course not.

Esme I'm sorry. You're right. (*She has suddenly conceded, and now she looks tearfully at Amy, not able to believe that she is back in the house.*) I see you there, Amy, and for the first time ever I am feeling nervous . . .

Amy Mum . . .

Esme I mean, I'm nervous but I'm also relieved.

The tension is resolved. Esme speaks more gently.

I've missed you . . .

Amy Me too.

Esme I've missed you so terribly. How long is it? It must be over six months. I keep reading in the papers about all your problems. And I've so longed to be able to talk. The whole thing's left me feeling so helpless.

Amy Yes, I've felt pretty helpless myself. (*She manages a brave grin but her eyes are beginning to fill with tears.*) I suppose you could say I've behaved like a coward. I couldn't help it. I went into my shell.

Esme Yes.

Amy It never lets up. Never. In fact, throughout it, I've not talked to anyone. I've just stayed with the children.

Esme How are they?

Amy The children are fine. (*She waves a hand impatiently.*) Oh, we just hide all the papers. We hope the other kids say nothing at school.

Esme She's some sort of Swedish film star?

Amy Yes.

Esme I'm afraid I'd never heard of her.

Amy You're in a minority of one. That's why the media has been so enthused. We've had them on the doorstep with cameras.

Esme Is it possible? She is really Swedish?

Amy I think so.

Esme Swedish! (*She looks away in disgust.*) How low can you get?

Amy She has this throaty sort of gurgle. A tan and tons of blonde hair.

Esme You've met her?

Amy (*nods*) She's kind of a brainless Heidi. This big open grin. A lot of 'Why can't we be friends?'

Esme Please!

Amy Why can't we be friends? 'Because you're sleeping with my husband. I think that's one thing that might just get in the way.' (*She is spirited, full of fight.*) But, oh no, she wants us in the communal sauna. If she had her way, the three of us would all be romping with twigs. I don't buy her dewy-eyed innocence.

Esme How could you?

Amy Oh, but she does have quite a good act. (*She looks at Esme a moment.*) But what's worst is that Dominic's bewildered. He's guilty.

Esme I'm sure he is.

Amy No. Truly. It's much, much worse than you'd think. Because he's lost. It's true. It's like he's spun off his axis. Most of the time, he acts like he's crazy. What's sad is, he doesn't even know what he wants. Things had been so much better. I promise. Since our wedding, it was odd, for the first time we were almost at peace. Deciding to marry . . . it helped to resolve things. And then this woman came out of the blue.

Esme is watching her, quiet, respectful.

Also, he's now this media monolith. They're turning out hundreds of programmes a year. Music. And chat shows. And videos. So he sets out at dawn and escapes to his work.

Esme Is he living in the house?

Amy Oh, sure, yes, we're living together. 'For the sake of the children'. Is that what they say? Not that it makes any difference. I never see him. Unless I walk by a telly. I can watch him on telly, if I so choose. (*She is in agony, paler than ever.*) I'm trying, but it's hard to stay steady. In any relationship you get cast in a role.

Esme I understand.

Amy Yes, I've played the strong one. And after a while that starts taking its toll.

Esme is about to reply. Amy interrupts, as if she doesn't want to hear.

Esme Well . . .

Amy And meanwhile you and I were no longer speaking . . .

Esme Darling, whose fault is that?

Amy And then I got wind of what's happening to you . . .

Esme (*dismissively*) Oh . . .

Amy I spoke to some people I know. The word is you're now in serious trouble. Well, tell me!

Esme Oh, sure, but mine's only money, that's all. (*She smiles blithely at Amy.*)

Amy Debts?

Esme Yes, of course.

Amy And are they substantial?

Esme I've really lost track of them . . .

Amy Mum . . .

Esme They change all the time.

Amy looks at her, not letting her off.

The last time I opened one of those envelopes, then, yes, it was quite a large sum.

Amy How much?

But Esme has already got up and is heading for the discarded envelopes.

Esme Hold on, now where are my glasses? Let's look at this one which just came today. Look, yes, it's not so unusual. (*She is holding the letter from the envelope some way from her glasses.*) It seems to be round about five.

Amy Five? Five what?

Esme Five hundred thousand.

Amy Mum . . .

Esme Five hundred thousand – or so. There are lots of smaller figures as well. Not *exactly* five hundred thousand. Something a little more jagged than that. (*She is peering in a rather actressy way which plainly irritates Amy.*) Or perhaps it's a six. It's all academic. It isn't the largest I've had. One morning, I simply couldn't believe it. I looked at it. It was eight! It was over eight hundred thousand. I thought this is just like being poked in the eye.

Amy Why are you laughing?

Esme My dear, what else can I do? The whole thing is just so totally . . . well, it's an out-of-body experience. What is the point of pretending it's real?

Amy But it is real.

Esme Yes. But – sorry – I simply don't have it. So what on earth do they want me to do?

Frank comes in triumphantly with a tray of hot drinks and biscuits.

Frank Cocoa!

Esme I mean, of course they can have what I give them . . .

Frank It's thick how you like it.

Esme I give them every penny I have.

Frank She does love it thick.

Amy But surely you don't have to go on paying for ever?

Frank Oh, Lord, are we on the forbidden subject again? (*He grins cheekily across the room.*)

Amy Is it true it's all down to asbestos?

Esme Asbestos! You name it. There's also this silicone they stick in womens' breasts . . .

Amy Silicone?

Esme Millions of American housewives . . .

Frank It's crazy . . .

Esme All suing their doctors. There's hurricanes.

Frank Called Hugo. Elyse. Victoria.

Esme That's right. Speeding through America, turning houses to matchsticks. In spite of their sweet little names.

Frank smiles up from stirring cocoa as Esme becomes more extravagant.

I tell you, whenever there's a serious disaster – you fall down, fall over, your house is burnt to the ground – in every country in the world, the procedure's the same, you turn to the victims and say: 'Don't fret, don't worry, there's really no problem. Just fill up a form and this weird British actress will pay!'

But Frank now wants to dissent.

Frank Oh, please now, my dear, you slightly exaggerate . . .

Esme Do I?

Frank There are plenty of syndicates doing much worse than yours.

Esme How can they do worse? I'm losing everything! How can you lose more than everything?

Frank Well . . .

Esme It simply doesn't make sense.

Amy But . . . I'm sorry . . . who chose these syndicates? Who actually decided which ones you were in?

Esme The man with the cocoa.

Frank is stirring the milky drinks. There is a moment's silence.

Frank It's true.

Amy You?

Frank Yes.

Esme You didn't know that?

Amy I suppose I'd never quite grasped it. You personally?

Esme Frank is a commissioning agent for Lloyd's.

Frank I am. I bring them their business. I find them their clients.

Amy I see.

Frank waits for what Amy will say next. It is a delicate moment.

I knew you did something financial . . .

Frank No, no, specifically.

Amy I knew you advised her.

Frank I did. I advised her in all sorts of ways. I took charge of her money. That's what I did for her.

Esme He has that unhappy distinction.

Frank That's right.

There is an awkward silence.

It was my job to place it. So you might say, in one sense, the whole thing's my fault.

Amy Yes.

Frank smiles as if this idea were absurd.

But I mean . . . you did warn her?

Frank Of course.

Amy You did explain all the risks?

Frank Please. There's no question. I did everything right. I did behave ethically. Impeccably. (*He leans in to Amy.*) Biscuits?

Amy No, thank you.

Frank It's a matter of simple bad luck.

Esme has sat down, content to let Frank explain. Frank seems equable, undisturbed.

Amy But the point is I also . . . I read in the paper there are certain people . . . it seems there's no limit to what they may owe.

Frank Yes.

Amy Is my mother one of them?

Esme Old Muggins. Wouldn't you know?

Frank seems unfazed.

Frank It's called unlimited liability. That's what is offered at Lloyd's. As a Name you put up money and then in return . . . one's exposure may literally be open-ended.

Amy I see. And my mother knew this?

Frank Oh, certainly, I'd say she was fully aware.

Amy's tone is lower, more dangerous.

I don't think it actually occurred to her . . . it didn't occur to any of the investors in fact . . .

Amy Quite . . .

Frank An eventual disaster might one day transpire. There were few signs.

Amy But . . . I don't quite know how to ask this . . . I suppose we can take it for granted . . . presumably you're in the same boat?

Frank looks to Esme.

Frank Well . . .

Amy Aren't you?

Frank Certainly, I do have some problems. I've taken bad losses. It hasn't been an easy period for me.

Amy But?

Frank But I was in a different spread of syndicates. This is all highly technical, but I do have a slightly different portfolio.

Amy I see.

Frank's manner is still mild. Esme is like a sphinx.

Frank It's a question of return for your capital. For a higher return you do take higher risks.

Amy And?

Frank Well, in my own investments I admit I was always more cautious.

A decisive moment has been reached. A few seconds pass before Amy speaks.

Amy More cautious with your own money, you mean?

At once Esme gets up.

Frank Now look . . .

Amy All right, I understand now, I understand what's happened . . .

Esme Frank, perhaps you should leave us. I was wondering, why don't you sleep here? We can talk again in the morning. (*She kisses him on the cheek.*)

Frank Yes. Whatever you say. (*He moves off towards the door. But when he reaches the door he turns back.*) Believe me, we all know that people are angry. When something goes wrong like this, it's human nature: you

94

want to lash out. But these things happen. There it is. They're part of experience. Now if you'll excuse me, I'm going upstairs.

He takes his cocoa and goes. As soon as he closes the door, Amy explodes.

Amy Oh, come on, I'm sorry, but this is outrageous . . .

Esme Oh, Amy.

Amy You know it is.

Esme Do I?

Amy Mother, it's just simple theft. You know what he's done to you.

Esme He hasn't done anything. No, it's simply too easy! I refuse to start saying that everything must be Frank's fault.

Amy It isn't his fault? When he's lost all your money . . .

Esme So?

Amy He's taken every penny you had! And did he ever mention . . . did he ever once mention that he was too nervous . . . no, he was too *clever* to take all the risks he was making you take?

Esme is trapped by the question.

Esme No. But, be fair, it's not something I ever asked him . . .

Amy Oh!

Esme The subject never came up.

Amy I bet it didn't!

Esme I refuse to start saying the whole thing's deliberate.

Amy My God, and this man who's destroyed you . . . you still let him sleep right here in the house!

Esme Why, of course. I'm allowed a companion.

Amy Yes, and, what's more, being Esme, you choose one who's actually ruined your life!

But Esme is already on the attack.

Esme I'm sorry, but the fact is, I did take their money.

Amy So?

Esme I used to get a cheque. I never refused it. It came in year after year. And – all right, you may think me con-temptible – but I always just thought of it as money for jam. (*She looks at Amy, unabashed.*) I would just sit there. Open the envelope. I got all this money. I loved it. I never thought twice.

Amy So?

Esme So – please – perhaps you'll excuse me if now I refuse to blame others. How can I blame anyone except for myself?

Amy frowns.

Amy But occasionally you must have had your suspi-cions . . .

Esme Oh . . .

Amy When the money just flowed in like that? Did you never think, hang on, there must be a catch here?

Esme Well, now you say it.

Amy Did you never think this is too good to be true?

Esme shrugs, insouciant.

Esme The stuff just rolled in like the ocean. The truth is, you do start to think it's your right. You get so you don't even notice. You just sort of think, 'This is nice. This is bound to go on.'

Amy But then when you started to lose some . . .

Esme Ah . . .

Amy Yes, when the losses began . . . then you must at least have considered, you must have thought it was time to get out?

Esme On the contrary. Frank used to say, oh good, look, there's been another plane crash, that's good for business, it helps remind everyone they ought to insure. (*She takes advantage of Amy's silence to try and make a joke of it.*) The only thing I would say . . .

Amy Yes?

Esme I actually noticed when I was a girl, all the thickest people one bumped into always seemed to be working at Lloyd's.

Amy Oh really!

Esme There was one chap I knew, even the Church wouldn't take him, but Lloyd's – oh, Lord yes, no problem at all. (*She laughs, stubbing a cigarette out.*)

Amy But all right, the point is, you knew you might one day lose *something* . . .

Esme Yes.

Amy You knew there was always that chance.

Esme Oh, sure.

Amy But did they actually stop and explain to you, 'Look, you can lose every penny you have?'

Esme seems exhilarated by the question.

97

Esme Oh, not just every penny. Amy, I don't think you've grasped it. I'm losing much more than that. If it was only everything I had at the moment, then – let's face it – that would be nothing at all. (*She stands, triumphant at her own logic.*) No, this is . . . well, this is more awesome.

Amy How?

Esme This is everything I'll ever earn. For ever. This is my whole working life. Whatever I do – whatever! – it doesn't make any difference. Do you really not get it? There's simply no end to the money I owe. I can work through the whole of the century. I can toil. When I'm dead I rise up and start tending the grass on my grave. I can work for the rest of eternity, but the simple fact is: I'll always be broke.

Amy tries to keep her focused.

Amy All right, but did anyone explain to you? Was this explained to you when you first joined?

Esme Oh, sure. I mean yes, very loosely.

Amy Mother, please tell me, was it or not?

Esme Yes. I mean, yes. Frank took me to London.

Amy And?

Esme We had a very good lunch. A really good lunch in the actual boardroom at Lloyd's. And the Chairman, well he'd seen my Ophelia . . . and the point is, he'd just loved it.

Amy moves away, really furious.

Amy I cannot believe this!

Esme And pretty soon after he gave me this form.

Amy This form?

Esme A consent form.

Amy shakes her head, irritable.

Fair enough, I admit I was flattered. I can't say I read it.

Amy You mean you just signed on the spot?

Esme I will swear to this day: this man really did love my Ophelia. He loved it. In that he was genuine. Whatever else may have been going on. (*And now she is angry too.*) All right, I can see! It's partly pure snobbery. If a cockney had said to me, 'You'll make all this money and you don't do a thing', I would have said, 'Hold on, I wasn't born yesterday.' So in a way, yes, I don't like to admit it, but it does boil down to a question of style. (*She waves helplessly round the room.*) You should see it. There are these big silver candlesticks. There is all this china and glass, stretching way down this fabulous oak-panelled room. All right, I can see it's England as sheer bloody theatre. But there are times when theatre's pretty hard to resist.

Amy But, Mother, it's no longer theatre. You might as well face it. Those days are gone. You yourself say it: that England is finished. This is the moment you have to fight back.

Esme looks at her, not understanding.

Esme Fight back? How?

Amy Well . . .

Esme Oh, no doubt you want me to start signing petitions?

Amy Yes . . .

Esme Start saying I'm not going to pay?

Amy Well yes, to begin with. I mean, that would be quite a good start.

Esme Go and sit on some awful committee? Go to

meetings in London where people talk about their money all the time?

Amy Mother, for the rest of your life, you'll be talking about money. Why not talk about getting some of it back?

Esme Join an action group? No, I don't think so. I don't think I want to be seen on a picket line with a load of judges and Tory MPs. No thank you. I'd much rather just take my punishment. I'll take my punishment and shut the hell up.

Amy Oh, I suppose you think that's so noble . . .

Esme No, I just think it's sensible.

Amy I suppose you think there's some kind of principle here.

Esme Well, I do. I do think principle comes into it. Yes.

Amy Then of course we all know there's no question. We have to accept it. Because we know what part principle plays in your life!

Esme looks at Amy suspiciously now, not sure what she means.

Esme Of course, I might do something if I thought it was worth it . . .

Amy Good.

Esme I'd start campaigning if I thought it would actually work.

Amy Well it will.

Esme So what should I do?

Amy The same as all the other victims. (*She pauses a second.*) You sue your agent.

Esme Sue Frank?

Amy Of course. It's essential.

Esme Oh, please, I do hope that's a joke.

Amy Why?

Esme Oh, come on . . .

Amy Even I . . . I've read in the papers . . .

Esme That's just the most crazy idea . . .

Amy Literally half of Lloyd's members are suing the bastards who got them into this mess. Why shouldn't you?

Esme I'd have thought it was obvious.

Amy Why should you be so different?

Esme Well, I suppose I'm just slightly inhibited by the fact we're meant to get married quite soon. (*She has shot this joke at Amy, but now she turns and points at Evelyn.*) And also . . . just think. Who looks after Evelyn? Who do you think pays for her nurse?

Amy Well . . .

Esme If it wasn't for Frank and his generosity, Evelyn would have long been living in one of those homes.

But Amy is not letting go.

Amy So what are you saying? That you're going to be Frank's prisoner for the rest of your life?

Esme No, of course not. I'm not Frank's prisoner.

Amy Aren't you?

Esme And Frank, may I remind you, is a very nice man.

Amy Oh yes, a nice man who's lost all your money.

Esme That's not who he is. It's just what he did.

Amy looks at her, amazed.

Amy We are what we do, for Christ's sake. Have you never grasped that? We are nothing else. There's no 'us' apart from the things that we do. (*She suddenly raises her voice, infuriated by Esme's unwillingness to fight.*) Mother, they're playing you. Do you not understand it? These people are crooks. They have posh manners, but at bottom they're just common criminals. And they feed off people like you! You know full well this is your moment. This moment isn't going to come twice. In your heart I think you do know that. You have to take control of your life.

Esme is suddenly provoked by this phrase.

Esme 'Take control'?

Amy Yes.

Esme What is this claptrap that all of you spout nowadays? Take control! As if our lives were like motor cars. Remember, I've never driven . . .

Amy Exactly!

Esme And what's more I never shall. (*She is blazing now, full of contempt.*) What a meaningless cliché! If you ask me why men always make such fools of themselves, it's because they're in love with the ludicrous notion that there's such a thing as to be in control! And now you want women to try it, you want them to peddle this same silly myth! Oh, you all say it so easily, so glibly! 'Take control of our lives'. Who's in control? Finally? I ask you. The answer is no one. No one! If you don't know that, you know nothing. It's children who shout, 'Look at me, I'm in charge . . .' Well, I just won't. I'm refusing. I hate the idea of whingeing. I hate the idea of not taking your medicine and saying, 'All right, I've had some bad luck. But that's life.' (*She goes across the room and sits down as if the matter were finished*.) You're not going to persuade me. So please let's change the subject.

There is a short silence.

Why are you looking like that?

Amy What, I'm meant to be charmed? Is that it? Is this some performance? My mother putting on this brave and gutsy display. Well, forget it! I'm not bloody charmed by it.

Esme Amy . . .

Amy Not in one single degree! (*She is moving towards Esme accusingly*.) On the contrary, I don't find it charming. I find it pathetic, you see. I've found it pathetic for the whole of my life. Because as long as I can remember you've done this.

Esme I've done what?

Amy You've pretended it's funny to live in a dream.

Esme is shocked at the depth of her daughter's anger.

'He just loved my Ophelia'! 'It's an out-of-body experience!' 'Oh, Lord, I suppose I never checked my accounts!' For Christ's sake, Mother, you're now in your sixties. Do you not think it's time you grew up? (*She gestures round the room*.) This incredible privileged existence! This exhausting performance! 'I'm an actress. Oh, Lord, I know nothing at all!' This prize-winning comedy with my cheerful, lovable mother. 'Oh, just show me the document. Where do I sign?' How long did you think you could do this? This refusal ever to admit or face the problems you have. When the means of solving them are there if you choose.

Esme Oh really?

Amy But no, of course you won't seize them. And why? Because you'd think it demeaning. Because you'd have to behave like everyone else.

Esme sees her chance to retaliate.

Esme Oh, I see, and you mean you've done so much better . . .

Amy No . . .

Esme You've lived your life so much better than me? This control you're so keen on – oh yes, you've mastered the rhetoric – sure, the rhetoric's easy! – but I've never noticed you actually exert it yourself. My God, you live with this man, this child, this figure who you think merits your love – and you let him run off with a slice of teenage Scandinavian *charcuterie* and even then – forgive me! – you don't even leave.

Amy Do you think I don't want to? Do you think I don't want to leave him today?

Esme Then please explain to me, tell me what's stopping you? (*She smiles at the obviousness of it.*) Is it the children or what?

Amy No. No, it isn't the children.

Esme What is it? Is it just dogged persistence? Is it because of Amy's famous view that love conquers all?

Amy No, it's not that.

Esme Then tell me what is it?

Amy What do you think it is? (*Suddenly she is in real distress.*) Because I can't face admitting you're right.

Esme stops, stunned.

Why do you think I've not called you? Why do you think we've not spoken for six months or more?

Esme I don't know.

Amy Because the moment I realized that I was in serious trouble with Dominic, then guess what? I realized I didn't want to speak to my mum.

   Esme is silenced, shocked.

You never gave him a chance. There's a side of Dominic that you never saw. That you never wanted to see. From the very first day you were determined to judge him. And now you've got what you want.

Esme That isn't fair.

Amy Isn't it? Do you think I haven't wanted to ring you? Every day I long to ring up the best friend I have . . .

Esme Oh, Amy . . .

Amy But every day I think I can't stand that moment, that look of pure triumph which I know I'm going to see in your eye! (*She smiles bitterly.*) You kept saying you looked down on Dominic. He worked in television, that's what you said . . .

Esme All right!

Amy You hated television because its values were poison . . .

Esme That's what I thought then.

Amy Oh, you'd have nothing to do with it . . .

Esme What do you want? I have to live somehow . . .

Amy But don't you see it's all so unfair? (*She suddenly laughs outright.*) You talk about your bloody TV show. Have I seen it? Have I seen it? I have. But only by wearing dark glasses, and with ear plugs stuck in both ears!

Esme turns away.

It's so typical. You lay out your principles. 'The theatre!'
Oh, and television's such a low form . . .

Esme Very well.

Amy And I swallow this stuff! And then your principles
turn out to be much more like prejudice . . .

Esme All right! Isn't that true of everyone?

Amy But because I believed it, I actually suffered. (*She
shows sudden satirical relish*.) At least with Dominic
there's something discussable. In what he does, there's
something there you can like or dislike. But Nurse
Banstead . . . my God, Nurse Banstead exhibits almost no
human features.

Esme Now, Amy . . .

Amy The show's beyond anything you can actually
debate. You stand there seriously arguing about whether
an operation's hygienic. Whether the show is authentic or
not. That doesn't depend, you know, on medical procedure. It depends on whether anyone has learnt how to
act!

Esme It's not bad. It's not badly acted. Some of the scripts
are a little bit weak.

Amy 'Nurse, I think I need an immediate tonsillectomy!'
'Doctor, I'm losing my amniotic fluid.'

Esme Now, Amy, this is just needlessly cruel.

Amy Is it? (*She is kind now, quieter*.) You never saw it.
Dominic was funny and gentle. Ambition's destroyed him,
that's all. Because he thinks that the world of the media
matters. He actually thinks that it's real. So it's been

harder to talk to him . . . for years it's been harder to reach him. It's true. So he's gone off with someone who cares about photos in magazines and opinion columns, and all of those dud London things. But that doesn't mean the man was always contemptible. It doesn't mean I shouldn't have been with him at all. It just means . . . oh, look . . . the odds were against us. But I happen to think it was well worth a try. (*Her anger has turned to distress, the tears starting to run down her cheek.*) Of course I knew . . . do you think I'm an idiot? I always sensed: one day this man will trade up. He'll cash me in and he'll get a new model. I always felt it would come. These men, they wait. They wait till they're ready. You make them secure. Then, of course, when you've built the statue . . . that's when they kick the ladder away. But I did know it. I did it knowingly. It was my choice.

Esme looks at her a moment.

Esme And are you parting?

Amy Why? Would you be satisfied?

Esme No!

There is a silence.

Amy You want us to part because then you're proved right.

There is a second's pause. Evelyn stirs and lets out a cry in her sleep. At once Esme gets up and tries to move to Amy.

Esme Oh, Amy, Amy please come and hold me . . .

Amy No, Mother . . .

Esme Amy, please, Amy . . .

Amy I can't . . .

Esme has reached her, wanting to put her arms round her, but Amy is backing away.

No . . .

Esme Come on, darling, you've always held me . . .

Amy I know . . .

Esme Since you were a child you've hugged me . . .

Amy I know but . . .

Esme Please come and hold me . . .

Amy I can't . . .

Amy has moved away. Esme, not really knowing what she's doing, pursues her.

I can't even sleep, I can't think, I'm in agony . . .

Esme Amy . . .

Amy What sort of mother? I want a mother who I can ring up.

Esme Please. Please come and hold me.

Amy Who I can call, who won't judge me . . .

Esme Amy, please stop this!

She has now put her arms round her, but Amy is struggling. For a moment the two women seem to be fighting, Esme holding on to her, Amy trying to escape her embrace.

Amy All you will say, all you'll ever say to me, 'Well guess what, my darling? I was right all along . . .' (*She suddenly shouts.*) I can't! I can't do this! Please let go of me.

Esme Amy!

Amy Please let go of me! Please!

It is suddenly shocking to both of them. Amy has thrown Esme violently off and stands, shaken by the passion of the moment. Evelyn stirs, groaning.

I went with Dominic because he was the future. I'm frightened of you because you're the past.

They look at each other across the darkened room. Amy starts to gather up her stuff.

Now I have to go . . .

Esme Please stay . . .

Amy No . . .

Esme Please stay.

Amy I'm sorry, Mother, I can't. Not tonight. I have to go back to London.

Esme I beg you, Amy, please stay.

Amy I can't. (*She looks, still unable to go near Esme.*)

Esme Please stay. Just tonight. Just stay here and comfort me.

Amy I can't. I have to get back. I have to . . . I have to just try and be steady. I have to.

They are both rooted to the spot.

Please let me. Mother. Please let me go. I have to.

Then Frank opens the door, and at once Amy moves quickly back towards the veranda.

I'll see you. I'll call you.

Esme Amy. Amy . . .

Frank I heard shouting. I heard you shouting downstairs.

Amy Goodbye.

Esme runs out towards the veranda and disappears, calling out.

Esme (*off*) Amy! Amy!

Frank What's happening?

There is a silence. Then the sound of a car starting out-side. Its headlights sweep through the room. Frank stands helpless, just waiting. After a few moments Esme returns. She does not look at him, but walks past him to go upstairs.

Esme Goodnight, Frank. Please lock the place up.

She is gone. Frank stands alone.

Act Four

London. 1995. The backstage of a small Victorian West End theatre. A small dressing room with a row of mirrors framed in lightbulbs. Esme has not done anything to decorate it at all, so the effect is painfully bare. There is just a stool and a surface for all her make-up. There is a small sofa and a screen. Some period costumes hang on a rail.

As the Act begins, Toby Cole is already appearing. He is in his early twenties, rather tousled and blithe. He has a Walkman round his neck, and a T-shirt, but he has not taken off his period breeches nor his dark make-up, so the effect is quite curious. He approaches the dressing-room door nervously and calls in.

Toby I'm sorry. Do you mind? (*A pause.*) Am I disturbing you, Esme? (*A pause.*) Are you sleeping?

Esme (*off*) If only.

Esme appears from behind the screen. She is now in her late sixties. She has been resting with her face covered in white cream, so that it makes a mask. She looks like a kabuki player. She wears a pink dressing gown. She seems withdrawn, as if she has retreated into herself. She goes to the door and opens it to let Toby in.

Oh, Toby, do you want to come in?

Toby I thought you might like a sandwich. I'm going to get a sandwich, that's all.

Esme smiles to say no, then goes to sit at her stool to begin getting ready for the next performance.

You never eat anything.

Esme throws a smile at him. Toby doesn't want to leave.

I was wondering what you thought of the matinee?

Esme Oh . . .

Toby I was pleased. It felt pretty good. I think I'm beginning to get the hang of that last scene. The rhythm. You always bang on about rhythm. And I thought this afternoon . . . well, actually the rhythm wasn't too bad.

Esme No.

Toby In that first scene, I wanted to ask: do I look too eager when you give me the apple?

Esme No, I think you do it just right.

Toby is hanging around the door, at ease.

Toby Did you hear the director's coming this evening?

Esme No.

Toby I'll be interested to hear what he thinks.

Esme says nothing.

I still can't believe it. It's incredible. I was thinking, I mean really . . . this honky little show. I stuck my nose out in the alley just now. There's already a great long queue for returns. I mean no disrespect to anyone, but it is quite amazing. Isn't it? I'm not being offensive but I never imagined it could happen to us. (*He smiles artlessly.*) I didn't dare tell you. I was telling my mother – this was weeks ago – you were going to star in this play. When she came to see it, she said – I didn't like to tell you – well, she said it was the best thing you'd ever done. (*He holds a hand up to avoid offence.*) You were always her favourite actress, I mean, not to be rude, but when she was young . . .

Esme It's all right.

Toby But she said . . . well everyone says this . . . it's like now you've got something extra.

Esme Perhaps.

Toby You should have heard her. She really meant it. She was really laying it on . . .

Esme carries on preparing.

Esme Do you get on with your mother?

Toby My mother? Oh, sure. I mean, my mother? Yes, absolutely. She's more . . . well, I never think of her as being like a relative. In fact I don't think of her as being my mum. You know, perhaps I'm lucky. Perhaps it's my generation, but to me my mum is more like a mate.

Esme Hmm. (*She is thoughtful a moment.*)

Toby Lately, you know, I've taken to watching you . . .

Esme I've seen you . . .

Toby I know. I just watch. When I'm not on, I stand in the wings and observe. I think . . . I don't know . . . it may be presumptuous but I feel I'm beginning to understand your technique.

Esme Good.

Toby You never play anything outwards. I've noticed you keep it all in. So you draw in the audience. So it's up to them. And somehow they make the effort . . .

Esme Yes.

Toby They have to go and get it themselves. (*He is embarrassed by his next question.*) What I don't know is, how do you do that? This sounds stupid. Do you learn it? Is there a secret? Some particular thing.

Esme No, I don't think so. (*She looks down a moment.*) It comes with the passage of time.

Toby Yes.

Esme You go deeper.

Toby Exactly.

Esme You go on down to the core. (*She shrugs slightly.*) There it is.

Toby I wish . . . I don't know . . . there were some way that we could all do it. Just do it, I mean.

Esme I shouldn't worry. I promise, for you it will come. Come here. (*She is very casual, but she has invited him over to kiss him lightly on the cheek.*) Maybe a small cappuccino.

Toby Of course. No really, this one's on me.

> *Esme has reached into her purse, but he is already on his way out. Esme goes out to her small bathroom beyond the screen. As Toby goes he passes Dominic, who has come into the corridor outside. Dominic is nearly forty. His boyishness has gone and his manner is more sober. He has thickened out to fill the smart, dark blue coat he is wearing. He is carrying a parcel the size of a shoebox, wrapped in brown paper. As he enters the room, Esme comes back, a slip showing underneath her untied dressing gown.*

Esme Dominic . . . (*Instinctively she wraps the dressing gown tight round her, holding herself.*)

Dominic I'm afraid I wandered in from the street. You seem to have no security.

Esme No. I think he goes off for a drink.

Dominic Ah. (*He shifts.*) I'm aware you don't want to see me. I've been hanging around for an hour. Just plucking up courage. I brought you a present.

Esme What present?

Dominic This. (*He puts the parcel down on the side. It is tied with string and sellotape.*)

Esme I need to prepare for the show. (*She sits down at her desk to start taking her mask of face cream off and to put on her make-up.*)

Dominic Actually I came to the matinee . . .

Esme Oh really?

Dominic Yes.

Esme No doubt you found it ridiculous.

Dominic Well . . .

Esme When did you last see a play?

Dominic shrugs.

Dominic Oh . . .

Esme I didn't hear you shout out 'fast-forward'.

Dominic No, to be honest, I was kind of intrigued.

Esme Just kind of? Not wholly?

Dominic Plainly the writer's so young.

Esme Yes he is.

Dominic That means it's absurdly pretentious. But then in a way I quite like that. I liked the play's youth.

Esme So do I.

Dominic That scene when you talk to the stars.

Esme throws a quick glance at him.

And somehow it's become this extraordinary phenomenon. Out of nowhere, it seems. Is that the appeal of the theatre in fact? This weird arty evening . . .

Esme Yes.

Dominic No one could ever predict it. And yet they fight to get in. (*He smiles at her a moment.*) What do you put it down to?

Esme What, this one?

Dominic The success of this particular play.

Esme Well, you're right, it's pretentious, it's true. And it's young. But I knew when I read it, it had something special.

Dominic You saw that?

Esme People like it because they feel it's sincere.

Dominic shifts, knowing he must somehow get past her coolness.

Dominic The children were saying you're in a small flat now . . .

Esme Yes.

Dominic You've moved back to London.

Esme looks at him sharply.

Esme But you knew that.

Dominic I did.

Esme You've sent me all those cheques . . .

Dominic Yes.

Esme I'm afraid they're no use to me.

Dominic I realized it must be in the terms of the settlement . . .

Esme I burnt them.

Dominic I guessed. (*He shifts again, uneasy.*) Well, the bank said they hadn't gone through.

Esme They couldn't.

Dominic No.

Esme The Hardship committee gives me an allowance. That's all I'm permitted. They seize all the rest. So unless you actually slip me a fiver, illegally . . . Whatever you give me, it goes back to Lloyd's. (*She is beginning to put her make-up on.*) I sold up the house, all my property, my furniture, my letters, my manuscripts. Everything I had. They take my wages. At the end I'm still short by two million. So, one way or another, your cheques aren't much use.

Dominic shifts again, moving towards what he has come to say.

Dominic I had thought it was personal, I'd feared you were angry . . .

Esme Oh really?

Dominic I feared you resented the money I sent.

Esme Yes, well, as I can't take it, I'm afraid you'll simply never find out.

This comes out so cold that Dominic tries to move on to the attack.

Dominic Look, Esme, I do know that you blame me . . .

Esme Blame you, you think?

Dominic You think in some way everything that's happened is somehow my fault. I know that. I know you hate my new marriage. In your shoes, that's something I well understand.

Esme I don't think of it, Dominic. I promise you. I do my best not to think about you at all. (*She smiles slightly in anticipation.*) Except when I see all your posters . . .

Dominic Ah yes . . .

Esme When I go down the tube. This film you've directed. Everyone says it's been winning all sorts of prizes.

Dominic Some.

Esme So it seems like at last you've done what you want.

Dominic is now slightly desperate to get through to her.

Dominic Look, the point is, I really am trying. I really am trying my best. Do you think I'm not changed by what happened? Do you think it hasn't changed me?

Esme says nothing.

You think I don't have any conscience?

Esme No.

Dominic You think it doesn't hurt me when the children tell me what they've seen of your life?

Esme My life?

Dominic Yes! They say you've completely retreated. Since Evelyn died, they say you see no one at all. You refuse to go out.

Esme So?

Dominic begins to get more forceful.

Dominic All right, you think I'm indifferent, I'm callous, you think I don't care, but somehow the thought of you suffering . . . The children say it's like you've given up trying.

Esme Oh really? They told you that? Is that how it seems?

But Dominic persists, not willing to be put off so easily.

Dominic They say you called off your marriage.

Esme Yes.

Dominic You were going to marry Frank?

Esme throws a glance at him.

Esme Since you ask. That was some time ago. A long time ago. But I did what Amy was always telling me.

Dominic I see.

Esme I decided to take my life in my hands. (*There's a moment's pause.*) There we are.

Dominic But you're alone now?

Esme Do you think this is really your business?

Dominic Well, as a matter of fact, I'm afraid that I do. Why do you think I've come here to see you?

Esme To be honest, I have no idea.

Dominic I came because everyone's worried. I wanted to see you were coping.

Esme Well, now you've seen me, so that's OK. (*She waits a moment, then goes on preparing.*) What, you're concerned for my welfare? Why? You have what you wanted. You've got a great family. The children tell me you've got a great wife. Why should it matter what on earth I am feeling? Dominic, do I really matter at all? (*She gestures vaguely outside the room.*) Any more than that dog out there in the alley? The sound of that train going by. That's all it is.

Dominic That is just nonsense.

Esme Oh, is it? The last thing that maybe might stop you sleeping. A source of minor discomfort in the otherwise perfect life you now live. (*She gets up and looks him straight in the eye. All her hostility towards him suddenly comes out.*) I did see the film. I'm appalled by the violence. I know in some way it's important to people like you. All that shooting and bloodshed. But I don't understand it.

Dominic We don't call it violence. We call it action.

Esme Whatever. It isn't how life is. Perhaps I'm just getting old. (*She looks at him, unrelenting.*) I'm tired of it, Dominic. This need you all have to get out the guns, and bam! and wham! and 'kill the little fucker' and 'shoot off his stupid bloody head'. What is it? What is this need you all have now? What happened? Are you just bored?

> *Dominic just looks at her, not answering.*

Or is it that you just don't dare to deal with real experience . . . with the things that really go on in real life? Like grief . . . and betrayal . . . and love and unhappiness . . . and loss . . . the loss of people we love . . . (*Her eyes now have filled up with tears. She is disturbingly out of control.*)

Dominic Esme . . .

Esme No . . .

> *Dominic has moved towards her in an instinctive gesture of sympathy, but she puts up her hands to prevent him.*

Loss. Yes, let that be your subject. Not childish games

with explosions and guns . . . Which have nothing to do with anything . . . nothing to do with things that are real . . . (*She cannot look at him. She turns and goes behind the screen and into the bathroom.*)

Dominic You know Amy's view: you have to love people. You just have to love them. You have to give love without any conditions at all. Just give it. And one day you will be rewarded. One day you will get it back.

Esme returns. She has put on a pair of ragged trousers and is buttoning a blouse. She is carrying a pair of shoes. She sits and starts to put them on.

At the end, the fact is – I don't expect you to like this – but Amy and I were getting on well. No, truly. We were. We came to some real understanding. Of course it's not . . . it wasn't like it was any longer a marriage. But we did manage some sort of real love.

Esme is silent, tense now.

After we'd split, admittedly. You may say it's easier. But it lasted, I don't know, three months. Or four. We were closer than at any time in our lives. So now . . . perhaps this is mad to you . . . but somehow the story just doesn't seem finished. Do you understand me?

Esme Of course.

Dominic I feel that now I must try and help you.

There is a silence.

Esme You want Amy's death to be of some use.

Dominic Yes. (*He waits a moment.*) Because she just died – just dropped dead from a haemorrhage – one day she walks down a street, for no purpose, for no reason at all – one day she's there, then she's not – I've felt since that day, I have to see Esme.

Esme Why?

Dominic I do have to talk to her.

Esme So that I can tell you it wasn't your fault?

Dominic No!

Esme Tell you you didn't betray her? That none of it mattered? Is that what you want?

Dominic No, of course I betrayed her.

Esme Well then.

Dominic I really don't think that's the point.

Esme No? (*She waits for him to go on.*)

Dominic I want you to say, all right, that was one chapter. And now that chapter is closed.

> *Esme sits down, saying nothing.*

It's just . . . it's ever since the funeral . . . I've had this feeling, this instinct, it's much more than grief. It's to do with what Amy would have wanted.

> *Esme looks down in as much pain as him.*

Amy would have wanted that we should be friends.

> *Esme cannot answer him.*

Surely? I mean, with time that is possible. For Christ's sake, you know what she felt. More than anything she wanted that you and I should somehow get on.

Esme Oh, I see . . .

Dominic Yes . . .

Esme You're saying you left her, you're saying you know you did let her down. But because Amy was good, because she was decent, somehow you shouldn't suffer? I have to forgive you because she was so much nicer than you?

Dominic doesn't respond.

Some people rise. Well, don't they? They rise at other peoples' expense. For them to rise other people go down. We have to endure that. But please don't expect us to like you as well.

Dominic You don't understand. I'm saying something much simpler. Something for your sake too. Something which means we'll both be forgiven. (*He looks down.*) Because hating me now is a waste of your life.

Esme looks at him a moment, as if genuinely considering this.

Esme I have my life here in this theatre. My life is when the curtain goes up. My work is my life. I understand nothing else.

She waves a hand slightly to fight tears, but Toby is already back with two cappuccinos. They are both piping hot and he is juggling them slightly.

Toby Coffee.

Esme Oh, Lord . . .

Toby I think it's still hot enough.

He puts the cappuccino down on the surface. Esme resumes getting dressed.

Esme Do you know Dominic here?

Toby Are you Dominic Tyghe?

Dominic Well, yes.

Toby I can't believe it. Wow! It's just incredible. I saw that film you just made.

Dominic Oh yes.

Toby The scene where the man's skull exploded! That shot of the flying blood and the bone . . . (*He mimes shooting himself, and the effect of the back of his head exploding.*) I thought it was absolutely fantastic.

Dominic Oh, well, thanks very much.

Esme looks at Dominic but Toby, drinking his cappuccino, does not notice.

Toby You're an old friend of Esme's?

Dominic I married her daughter.

Toby Ah yes.

Dominic We go back a long way. But she died very tragically. Without any warning.

Toby waits a second, respectful.

Toby Esme did mention. Do you have children?

Dominic We do.

Toby How are they coping?

Dominic By and large, they cope very well. (*He throws a glance at Esme.*) And they both love their granny.

Toby Yes. Well, we all love her here too.

Esme does not want this attention. She busies herself with getting ready.

Look, you know we only have three minutes.

Esme What? I don't believe you.

Toby It's true.

Esme I didn't hear the call. I must have missed it.

Toby Excuse me.

Toby slips out the door.

Esme Dominic, you will have to go now.

Dominic Will you think about what I've been saying?

Esme I'll try to. Yes. If I can.

Dominic waits patiently. Esme moves towards her coffee and takes a sip.

That day I remember so clearly. The day I walked in. You'd been mending the bike.

Dominic Yes.

Esme What was my reaction? Was it just fear of the stranger?

Dominic Only you know. Is that what it was?

Esme My daughter was lost to me. One look at you. Everything I had left to me was gone. Do you think it was pure blind instinct?

Dominic No. To be fair, you did dislike me personally too.

They smile together, some real warmth between them for the first time.

Esme It was just chance. It was chance I met Bernard. I was promiscuous. I was also nineteen. In angora sweaters and little short skirts. But I met this man. And from then on, everything seemed to be different. What if I hadn't? It was pure luck. (*She stands, lost in thought.*) Life with Bernard wasn't actually spectacular. It wasn't as if we were always in each other's arms. It was just calm. And we laughed at everything. That's all. Nothing crazy. But always with him, I felt whole.

There is an offstage call of 'Beginners, please'. Dominic takes a couple of steps backwards, pointing to the parcel.

Dominic Remember, open your present. (*He stops at the door.*) Esme, will you promise to call me?

Esme If I could, then why would I not?

Dominic goes out. Esme is alone. She reaches up to the tannoy, and the sound of the waiting audience is heard. She adjusts her costume in front of the mirror. She looks a moment at herself, then, curious, she takes the parcel he's left. She opens a drawer and takes a knife out. She cuts the string. She pulls back the paper. It's a shoebox. She opens it. Inside it are bundles of five pound notes – thousands of pounds' worth. She shakes her head, and puts the lid loosely back on. As she does, Toby returns with a jug of water. He sees her closing the box.

Toby What was that?

Esme My daughter's ashes.

Toby looks puzzled.

Take no notice. It's a gift.

She picks up the box and, in a sudden gesture, throws it into a cupboard below the shelf. Then briskly she closes the door. She checks herself once more and leaves the room with Toby and they walk together towards the stage. The dressing room disappears. When they get to the stage then silently, without any prompting from her, she leans down, half forward, and he pours the jug of water over her head, soaking her hair and the top half of her body. She smiles at him.

Thank you.

Toby starts taking off his T-shirt.

Toby Oh, by the way, the director's not coming.

Esme Oh really?

Toby No, he's changed his mind. He's not coming.

He has taken off his trousers. He has just a strip of cloth round his middle, barely covering him, and he looks pitiful, like Poor Tom in King Lear. She pours the rest of the water from the jug over him, and he shivers. She hands the jug to a stage manager. Then they stand together a moment, he blue with cold, she already focused on the task ahead, both of them curiously innocent in the silence.

Esme Fair enough then. So we're alone.

The light begins to go down, until it is only on the two of them, glazed, nervous, full of fear.

Suddenly there is the overwhelming sound of a string orchestra and the light goes down to near-blackness. Then they turn towards us, and the curtain goes up.